ECube Leadership©

THE POWER OF EMPATHY, EXUBERANCE, AND EXECUTION

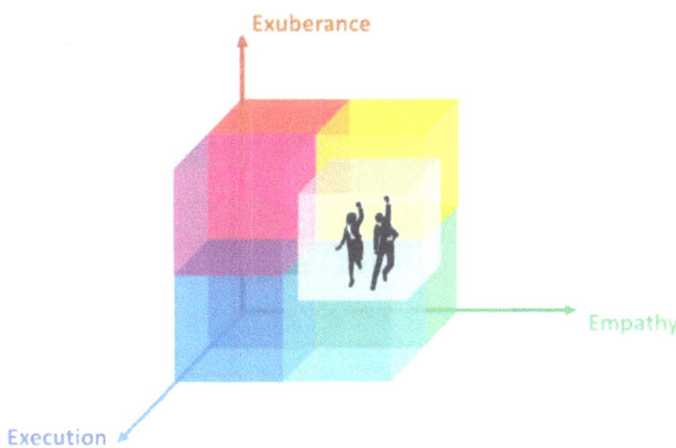

GEORGE KOSHI

Clever Fox PUBLISHING
Chennai • Bangalore

CLEVER FOX PUBLISHING
Chennai, India

Published by CLEVER FOX PUBLISHING 2024

Paperback ISBN: 978-93-67076-11-8
Hardback ISBN: 978-93-67070-15-4

This book is dedicated to my:

Dad, *who taught me that giving is greater than receiving,*
And to fail is fine if there is learning.
His memories may be fading away, but his wisdom
is here to stay.

Mom, *who has been through hardships with courage*
and grace, ensured I live in comfort, with the
lessons in place.

Anooja, *an amazing partner and guide, offering*
support and love and staying by my side.

Tarun & Abhinav, *who took me to my past, showing me*
millennial ways and memories that last.

FOREWORD

This book is appropriately timed.

These days, interpersonal relationships are constantly taking their cues from a social media influenced world. A world that is increasingly direct, quite often devoid of empathy and sometimes, devoid of context. The problem compounds itself when the environment is a professional set up.

ECube Leadership seeks to first clarify the equation by detailing what comprises effective leadership in an evolving world. Through multiple reference points, ECube Leadership reflects George's deep insights into the three essential pillars of leadership: Empathy, Exuberance, and Execution.

By focusing on these core elements, George encourages us to cultivate a leadership style that not only drives results but also inspires teams and nurtures talent. In a world where the traditional command-and-control model is rapidly becoming obsolete, the principles laid out in ECube Leadership are both timely and essential. This book challenges us to rethink our methods and embrace a more inclusive, energetic, and action-oriented approach to leadership.

I would recommend the book and its methodologies to aspiring leaders, seasoned executives, and anyone who seeks to make a meaningful impact within their organization. As you explore the pages of ECube Leadership, I hope you find inspiration and actionable insights that will enhance your own leadership journey.

Raju Vegesna
Chairman and Managing Director
Sify Technologies

PREFACE

For years, I have been contemplating authoring a book. While I had numerous ideas, focusing on one and elaborating on it proved to be a challenge. I am not good at crafting fiction, and I knew my strength lay in writing about concepts. Thus, a non-fiction book on a management topic seemed ideal.

I wanted to cover topics that would benefit readers both personally and professionally. As an educator and learning specialist, I began writing a book about teaching and learning methodologies for an audience in the education sector. Despite starting with great enthusiasm, my interest faded after a few pages, and I eventually abandoned writing this book.

Then a new idea emerged: writing about atheism, with the working title of 'Blank.' I anticipated that this could be a controversial and sensitive subject. However, I found myself stuck on the tenth page of 'Blank,' feeling uninspired and unable to continue as I felt blank.

My inner voice questioned whether I had the discipline to write consistently enough to complete a book. I realized that writing a book demands a great deal of dedication. Around the same time, I developed an interest in open-source technologies and began exploring Linux distributions like Ubuntu, Linux Mint, and Fedora, along with applications such as WordPress, OBS, and Ardour. This led me to create a personal website, https://georgekoshi.com. To keep the site active, I needed to publish content regularly, so I decided to start a blog, where I began writing articles on topics that piqued my interest.

I doubted my ability to maintain the discipline needed to write a book, but I realized I could write short articles on management or other topics and publish them as blog posts. This seemed like a more achievable goal.

I started writing blogs on leadership, based on my experience at work in various organizations, which eventually became my favourite topic. These blogs helped me to share my thoughts and opinions with my friends and colleagues, on various concepts of leadership and the attributes associated with good and bad leaders.

The journey of writing blogs inspired the creation of this book.

I would like to thank my wife Anooja George, who took the challenging task of editing this book. Her patience and sharp attention to detail has been invaluable in bringing this book to life. I am truly grateful.

TABLE OF CONTENTS

INTRODUCTION

Millions of books and countless articles have been written on leadership and are available in bookstores under self-help or management sections. Given the high demand for leadership skills, exploring various perspectives on this topic can be quite fascinating.

In my role within Learning & Development(L&D), leadership development is one of the Key Result Areas (KRA) amongst others like content management, behavioural and technical training to manage performance of the L&D function. I have conducted numerous training sessions for leaders, covering topics such as Building High Performance Teams, Emotional Intelligence, Coaching, Presentation Skills, Critical Thinking and Design Thinking.

Only a few leadership concepts offer both a model and an assessment tool. One of the most valuable models I have encountered is the People-Oriented vs. Task-Oriented matrix, which later evolved into the Situational Leadership framework. This model emphasizes that no single leadership style is ideal; instead, leaders adapt their approach based on the maturity of their team and the situation.

Another intriguing model is the Leadership Dimensions survey, built around four interrelated competencies: profound knowledge, profound strategy, purposeful direction, and purposeful behaviour. I found the 180-degree assessment to be particularly effective for coaching and training.

As an MBTI practitioner, I have leveraged the insights from the Step II Interpretive report, to guide and develop leaders. By assessing whether the extraverted or introverted mental functions are primary or weakest, I use these findings as a diagnostic tool for leadership development.

I explored various leadership theories like Charismatic Leadership, Transformational Leadership, and Servant Leadership. However, these concepts were largely theoretical. I could not find any structured models or psychometric assessment tools based on these leadership theories for practical use in training and coaching.

This realization led me to consider developing a simple Leadership Model with an assessment tool that would add value to the existing leadership literature.

The purpose of writing this book, *ECube Leadership*, is to present a new perspective on leadership through a framework built on three core attributes.

The key takeaways from this book are:

1. A visual classification of leadership styles based on the three core ECube leadership attributes.
2. A psychometric assessment to help evaluate yourself.
3. Insights from the collection of blogs I have written on leadership.

I have included ten blogs in the later chapters, each discussing various attributes and qualities of different types of leadership.

Although I have used the terms "Organization/s" and "Institution/s" to illustrate leadership concepts and examples throughout the book, they are not limited to the corporate world. Please interpret them in relation to your own workplace and the environment in which you operate.

I am pleased to have completed this book, and I hope it will be a valuable resource for leaders, managers, teachers, trainers and coaches in developing future leaders.

CHAPTER 1

THE NEED FOR LEADERSHIP DEVELOPMENT

One of the most frequently asked questions in leadership workshops is, "Who is a leader?" Despite the many responses available in books and training sessions, and the extensive knowledge on this topic, there remains a shortage of effective leaders in organizations, institutions, and governments. This suggests that, although we have abundant information on leadership, only a few individuals apply these principles to transform themselves into effective leaders.

This does not mean we lack capable leaders; we do have them, but we need more.

How often have we wished for the people collaborating with us in leadership positions, to be strategic, decisive, people-oriented, empathetic, fun-loving, and friendly?

Why is there a scarcity of good leaders?

Here are some thought-provoking questions to ponder:

- Do all organizations and institutions evaluate their employees for leadership competencies before assigning them leadership positions?
- Do all organizations and institutions have a leadership development process in place to build a strong pool of leaders for effective succession planning?
- Are leadership development initiatives integrated into the curriculum of schools and colleges to shape future leaders?
- Should leadership skills be a prerequisite for political candidates?
- Is the lack of leaders in our country a result of not having a clear long-term vision and a structured approach to leadership development?

Unlike elections, where voters have the power to choose their leaders, employees in organizations have no say in selecting their leaders. As a result, we often cannot choose our bosses.

We elect legislators and parliament members based on political party propaganda and manifestos, rather than evaluating their leadership qualities. Voters typically choose candidates based on popularity and personal biases rather than their values and leadership abilities. In any democratic country, voters must recognize their rights and the power they hold in selecting capable and effective leaders.

In both organizations and governments, individuals sometimes advance due to their tenure, loyalty, and political maneuvering while their leadership capabilities are frequently overlooked. While it is important to provide growth opportunities for employees, it is equally crucial for individuals to actively acquire and develop the necessary skills to become effective leaders.

We seem to lack the foresight to create an environment and infrastructure that supports the growth of leaders, which is essential for building strong organizations and institutions.

Unfortunately, only a handful of organizations and institutions invest the necessary resources – money, time, and effort – into leadership development.

Some large progressive organizations often have leadership academies with the primary goal of developing future leaders. This development is facilitated through assessment centers, coaching, and training programs.

Typically, these organizations allocate around 1 to 5 per cent of their total revenue towards leadership development initiatives.

Why would these organizations invest in developing leaders?

Organizations that invest in leadership development, recognize the importance of succession planning to avoid future failures. They are aware of the drawbacks of lateral hiring, such as cultural mismatches, longer integration periods, and higher recruitment and training costs. Therefore, nurturing leaders within the organization is crucial to retain top talent.

This approach to leadership development should extend to schools, colleges, and small to medium enterprises. It is crucial to establish dedicated programs for cultivating leaders in all areas, rather than depending solely on their organic growth within the system.

Leadership across Domains

The dynamics of leadership are different in different fields. Leadership in different domains must be treated and approached differently.

As the saying goes, leaders are made, not born. Also, leadership is not limited to those with formal titles only – it is accessible to everyone.

The ECube Leadership framework highlights the high-level attributes of a leader that are applicable across various professions. However, the specific functional and technical skills needed to excel in different fields vary and must be developed through dedicated effort and practice.

Whether you are in a leadership role at work, a professor or teacher, an entrepreneur, a salesperson, an accountant, a lawyer, a doctor, an individual contributor, an artist, an entertainer, or an athlete, the principles of ECube leadership can resonate with you.

CHAPTER 2

UNDERSTANDING OUR FACULTIES

Let us begin with the fundamentals of how humans think, feel, and react in various situations. Understanding the process of thought generation and interaction is crucial for leadership development.

Humans possess three key faculties: Thinking, Feeling, and Reacting. These can be directed inwardly towards oneself or outwardly towards others, events, or the environment. How we Think, Feel, and React about ourselves (inward) and towards others, events, or the environment (outward) can differ from person to person, influenced by the specific event and environment.

These dynamics make personalities different from each other.

Faculties of a Human Being

1. The ability to Think,
2. The ability to Feel, and
3. The confidence to React

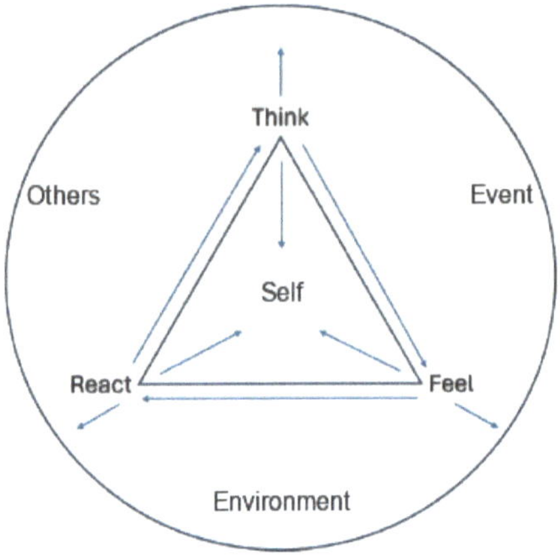

Figure 1.0. Faculties of a Human Being

In all situations, our communication and behaviour are based on the faculties of thinking, feeling, and reacting. The way we communicate and behave can influence others positively or negatively. This influence is powerful and is deeply rooted in an individual's personality, culture, and value system.

> *"The happiness of life depends on the quality of our thoughts."*
>
> **– Marcus Aurelius**

Leadership as a skill should be analyzed and researched from fundamental perspectives, such as the evolution of human beings; our ways of thinking, feeling, and reacting; and the influences of history, religion, culture, and scientific advancements. All these factors have shaped the way leaders think, feel, and behave.

In ancient times, strength and courage were viewed as the most vital qualities of a leader. Individuals who demonstrated these traits and conquered lands through their might and military power were celebrated as great rulers. As knowledge and wisdom gained importance, strategic kings and queens emerged, becoming even more powerful. Eventually, the emphasis on strength and courage diminished, giving way to a leadership model focused solely on intellect, knowledge, and wisdom. Today, corporate leaders, scholars, and scientists exemplify this type of leadership, while strength and strategy have shifted to the realm of sports and armed forces.

In recent times, compassion and empathy have become top leadership competencies. The importance of Emotional Intelligence (EI) over traditional intelligence is highlighted in all leadership literature.

> *The quality of our thoughts depends on our value system and belief system.*

Integrating values into leadership skills is essential. In my first blog on leadership, titled "Who is a Real Leader?" I delve into this value-skill integration. The positive feedback and responses from readers motivated me to further explore this topic and you will read more on this in the coming chapters.

Leadership is relevant across all fields, including organizations, institutions, governments, armed forces, and religion. While the styles of leadership may vary in each context, the core attributes of effective leadership remain consistent.

Animal, Man and Leader

How are we different from other animals? Aren't we fundamentally the same, as members of the Kingdom Animalia, Genus Homo, and Species sapiens? The difference is that Homo sapiens evolved more quickly, becoming more intelligent, social, greedy, and cunning.

Despite the advancements in our intellect and emotional intelligence compared to other species, there are still times when we fail to show respect and consideration for our fellow humans and other living beings.

Humans inhabit the concrete jungle, while our fellow creatures live in the natural jungle. The dynamics of domination and nurture are similar in both. However, the key difference is that humans have grown greedier, and their desire for power and control has made them worse than other creatures.

We share the same instincts as other animals—the urge to dominate and the instinct to nurture. A good leader nurtures and fosters an environment that benefits future generations without imposing their beliefs. Leadership is fundamentally about striking this balance, between nurturing and control.

How can we measure success in leadership?

Is leadership solely about attaining the top positions in organizations, institutions or governments?

Reaching the pinnacle of a department or an organization may not be the only measure of leadership success. It is not uncommon to see individuals in high-ranking roles who may lack the essential skills or attitude for effective leadership.

Instead of prioritizing governance, fostering growth, developing infrastructure, industries, agriculture, and enhancing education and healthcare, some government leaders at the city, state, and national levels become involved in political manoeuvring, corruption, and spreading false propaganda.

Similarly, some corporate leaders may get entangled in corruption and power struggles.

We also have spiritual leaders who position themselves as heads of various cults and religious groups, wielding significant influence over their followers. While their mission should ideally be to spread love and positivity, they often seem more intent on expanding their religious and political enterprises.

The question arises: Are they truly leaders?

Do you think their leadership style reflects positive values and moral principles?

We all know the answer to that.

True leadership requires shifting focus from personal growth to the development of others. The transition from self-centric to people-centric leadership is deeply rooted in a leader's value system.

So, leadership is shaped by our thoughts, emotions, and reactions in different situations, which forms our core personality. It is also influenced by the knowledge we gain through our experiences and how we cultivate our beliefs and value systems. One of the critical measures of leadership success would be based on the positive and outcome-oriented decisions leaders make during their career.

Here are the four questions this book explores on leadership:

1. What personality traits distinguish effective leaders from ineffective ones?
2. What skills must be acquired and developed to transform an average leader into an effective one?
3. What are the different styles of leadership?
4. How can we define and measure these various leadership styles?

The ECube Leadership describes different styles of leaders based on few chosen attributes. The idea of incorporating a tool to measure these attributes and thereby align different styles of leadership with each individual came from the fundamental questions mentioned above. I am sure many of us are eager to evaluate ourselves and discover which leadership style aligns with us.

CHAPTER 3

THE ECUBE LEADERSHIP ATTRIBUTES

The rule of threes has always proven to be powerful. Communicating any message with three points or stories makes it clearer and more impactful. So, I chose to create a leadership model with just three attributes. I believe that this would keep the model simple, yet powerful.

What could these three attributes focus on?

The primary objective and need is that these three attributes should encompass all essential leadership competencies.

The first attribute could emphasize individuals and teams, as a leader's primary role is to develop those around them. The second could focus on goals and deadlines or overseeing a business operation efficiently. The third attribute might focus on the energy, enthusiasm, and spontaneity required to motivate and drive both people and the organization forward.

After thorough research and reflection, I identified the top three attributes essential for effective leadership to be **Empathy, Exuberance,** and **Execution**.

Some of the thoughts that led me to this conclusion came from my experience in training and coaching individuals and from various psychometric tools:

- Value systems are crucial in defining a true leader. While Empathy has been selected as a core value component, other values like honesty, generosity, and transparency can be more difficult to measure to provide reliable or near-accurate results through psychometrics.
- Most key leadership competencies can be grouped into these three attributes. Interestingly, some competencies require a combination of two or even all three attributes, adding to the model's robustness. For instance, problem-solving skills require a mix of Empathy, Exuberance, and Execution attributes, while collaboration skills require a blend of Exuberance and Empathy.
- Many popular leadership assessment tools emphasize two critical skills – people skills and task skills. While people skills include team collaboration and empathy, and task skills include execution and business acumen, the importance of a third dimension – energy, enthusiasm, and spontaneity – has become increasingly evident. Interestingly, this attribute also tends to exhibit more observable and identifiable behaviours.

Therefore, using attributes that are simpler to assess and define and may not have interdependence with other attributes would make for a more effective model.

To elaborate on the three identified attributes, I wrote a three-part blog series, titled:

1. An Empathetic Leader: A Scarcity
2. An Exuberant Leader: A Necessity
3. Strategic Execution Skills in a Leader: A Priority

You will find these three blogs covered in detail in the following three chapters.

My experience working with senior professionals across various industries, combined with the insights from my blogs, inspired the creation of this leadership framework.

CHAPTER 4

AN EMPATHETIC LEADER; A SCARCITY

As a learning consultant, I have collaborated with managers and leaders, helping their teams develop relevant behavioural and functional competencies.

During this journey, I have engaged with many senior professionals, who were business heads, heads of departments and functions, and those managing large teams. Working with such leaders helped me evaluate and understand different leadership traits.

Based on my educated guess after analyzing their behaviours, I can say that only a handful of these leaders were empathetic. Empathy as we all know is an inevitable trait of a leader.

It is the ability of the leader to connect with people, on a human level and see beyond one's circumstances, which is key to Emotional Intelligence.

In his books on Emotional Intelligence (EI), Daniel Goleman highlights empathy as a crucial skill for effective leadership. Yet, this vital quality is one that many leaders often lack.

Is leadership about controlling people?

We all know the answer to this question, and sadly, this is what most people in leadership positions do, control people. Good leadership is all about developing people. A so-called leader may use the power of one's position to control people, but a true leader uses the power of empathy and knowledge to develop people.

The adage of putting yourself in somebody's shoes may hold good for a definition, but it may not cut ice when it comes to demonstrating empathy. Empathy, in action, is being vocal and communicating the identified feelings of others.

Who is not an empathetic leader?

You will find many non-empathetic leaders in higher positions across various functions, who continue to frustrate their team members and customers due to their behaviours.

Here is an effort to categorize non-empathetic leaders based on their actions and behaviours. I am sure you would relate and identify with some of them, those you may have come across in your career.

Disclaimer: "All leaders and events in this blog are non-fictional and are based on incidents from personal experiences. Any similarity to a living or dead person may be true and warrants behavioural change."

The Know-it-Alls

There is always a person of this kind in most teams. Listening is a big part of being empathetic. The know-it-all leaders love to listen to their own voices and hence are bad listeners. When leaders are the know-it-all type, they become over-involved and display their shallow knowledge in all the discussion points.

They sometimes go into a repetitive mode, like a broken record, annoying their team members.

One-size-fits-all; is what they follow. Be it any scenario, the know-it-all would come up with their concept and would try and fit it into the scenario.

I once had to deal with a leader who always said, "Opinions are the lowest form of knowledge." When opinions come from the top management, then conformity bias set in. Conformity bias conforms to people who have authority, power, and status, leading to agreeing to their opinions. When the same opinion came from the junior employees, it was discounted or discarded by quoting his favourite phrase.

The Belittlers

Appreciation is scarce from these leaders. The Belittlers enjoy overly criticizing and putting their team members down, even if they do exemplary work.

They fail to realize that genuine appreciation is the best way to motivate their team.

Even if one writes good emails or delivers excellent presentations, it is trivialized as just 'English'. These managers do not invest their time in coaching their team members but love to swoop in when a mistake is committed, only to blame. How easy is that?

The Control-Freaks

Some senior executives are control freak leaders who do not empower their team managers.

They micromanage every task of the various teams under them and do not allow the respective managers to make decisions for their teams. They insist on having the final say in every discussion and decision. This behaviour demotivates managers and undermines team morale.

Control-freak leaders tend to hold on to the harness of every individual, even at the lowest levels. In doing so, they fail to recognize that the larger team, responsible for driving the organization forward, is being pulled in different directions rather than working toward a common vision or goal.

The Conceited Boss

Team members who work under a conceited boss do not have a say in any topic discussed.

Even if meetings are conducted to brainstorm, all ideas from team members are shot down. Then the boss comes up with his own ideas and it becomes the chosen one to be implemented. Most decisions made by this kind of bosses are ego-driven and self-opinionated.

It does not matter whether the team members are experienced, experts or novices, the boss has the final say and is closed to suggestions and opinions from the rest of the team.

The conceited boss may sometimes be passively aggressive, and their aggression may not be very conspicuous and is usually expressed indirectly.

The Repercussions

Non-empathetic leaders drive away talents and are detrimental to the organization. They bring down the morale of the team, leading to dysfunctional teams.

Hence, employees working with non-empathetic leaders would carry on work with despise. They will keep looking out for better employment elsewhere for a quiet quitting.

Many of you may wonder as to how these leaders reach the top levels with this non-empathetic behaviour and display of negative attitude.

Often, individuals advance in an organization based on their tenure and individual performance, becoming leaders primarily due to their titles. Some may also secure positions through relationships, without being assessed on relevant skills.

So, organizations should re-look at the process of hiring and promotions especially while filling leadership roles where people management skills are of utmost importance. They also need to invest in training leaders in Emotional Intelligence to curtail attrition and improve engagement. In the current times, it becomes imperative as these leaders manage more millennials than Gen X as team members.

Questions to consider: Does your organization have a robust leadership development plan? Do they invest in training the leaders on Emotional Intelligence?

I conducted a poll to understand the prevalence of non-empathetic leaders in the workplace.

The question posed was: "Which type of non-empathetic leaders have you come across the most in your work or business environment?" The options provided were:

- The Belittlers
- The Control Freaks
- The Know-it-alls
- The Conceited Boss
- All the above
- None of the above

The poll results were quite revealing: 46% of respondents indicated that they had encountered all these types of non-empathetic leaders in their organizations. This was followed by 17% who had primarily come across Belittlers, 15% who had dealt with Control Freaks, 13% who had encountered Know-it-alls, and 8% who had faced Conceited Bosses. Interestingly, no one chose "None of the above."

CHAPTER 5

AN EXUBERANT LEADER; A NECESSITY

There are no shortcuts to building trust. Leaders should learn to build trust through continuous and honest engagement with their team members. The engagement must either be empathetic or exuberant, which helps in the trust-building process.

'An Empathetic leader; a scarcity', in the previous chapter, talked about the importance of empathy, as a critical skill for leaders. In this chapter, I would like to focus on another attribute that helps in leadership development, Exuberance.

Have you seen people becoming cheerful and lit up because a leader walked in? Everybody looks up to this leader because of the charisma and energy this person bestows.

The contrary also happens.

We may have seen when some leaders walk in, the energy in the room instantly vanishes. Chitter-chatter to silence, laughter to gloominess, hope to despair, optimism to pessimism.

What sort of a leader do you want to be?

Do you want to be a leader who energizes people around you or the one who sucks out all the energy? The latter is despised by all, but a leader with exuberance is always appreciated and is sought after.

When would you call a leader exuberant?

Enthusiasm, Energetic, Excitement, Liveliness, and Cheerfulness are synonyms for exuberance.

Leaders who combine passion, fun, and energy in everything they do and whose words and deeds are comfortable and pleasant to others, are Exuberant Leaders. They bring the element of passion to their work, and this is contagious, and the whole team becomes positive and enthusiastic about their work.

Team members become enthusiastic and willingly and happily collaborate with such leaders. So, exuberant leaders can easily mobilize teams and motivate them for strategic execution.

Characteristics of Exuberant Leaders

There are many ways to bring energy and passion to work. Some of the characteristics that help in the making of exuberant leaders are being an articulate leader, a happy-go-lucky leader, and a dapper leader. It is a good mix of all these attributes that make an exuberant leader.

An Articulate Leader

The most critical and conspicuous skill for leaders is the way they communicate. It is essential for leaders to communicate with impact and not be overly loquacious or taciturn in their interactions.

Loquacious leaders are overly talkative and sometimes speak without any relevance or need. Taciturn leaders are reserved and do not communicate enough. An articulate leader must have a good balance and should communicate right with vitality, brevity, and clarity.

Leadership skill is not just one skill but a set of many skills and abilities. One of those skills is to influence people. According to Robert B Cialdini, an American Psychologist, there are six ways to influence people. Being a positive role model and being likeable is one of the ways to influence people. How can one influence people without being an articulate leader?

A Happy-go-lucky Leader

In one of the surveys, 65 per cent of people said that it is important to have fun at work. All work and no fun would make anybody a dull person. Moreover, all fun and no work would also be useless. So, there must be a good balance between fun and work.

It becomes critical for leaders to bring the right amount of fun to work. One may come across leaders who are profoundly serious and sticklers for rules and regulations. It often becomes difficult for people to work with such leaders.

A team is made up of members who have different personalities. The leader must cater to all these personalities and help them advance in their career. A happy-go-lucky or an easygoing leader can build camaraderie, which subsequently would motivate each team member. If you are a senior person in an organization and managing a team, ask yourself this question; Do I bring in the fun at work? Am I a happy-go-lucky leader?

A Dapper Leader

A dapper leader dresses for the occasion; is casual when needed, business-like at meetings, bright at parties, and in sportswear when playing their favourite game.

Some might believe that dressing appropriately is not crucial and that only results matter. However, presenting oneself well is vital as it creates a positive first impression. Psychology suggests that first impressions are lasting, leading to a phenomenon known as Confirmation Bias, where individuals hold onto their initial judgments and perceptions about a person, event, or a belief, potentially disregarding new information that contradicts those initial views.

Results cannot be achieved without branding, positioning yourself, and making yourself visible. A dapper leader who is happy-go-lucky and can articulate well can do just that.

Exuberance must be woven into the culture of organizations, and this often cascades from the top. It is one of the primary and most important attributes that leaders should develop when working with teams.

Leaders who are naturally introverted might have to flex their personality type, to be exuberant. It takes a little bit more effort to be exuberant, compared to naturally outgoing and extroverted leaders. Doing so will help improve the leader's charisma and amiability, a necessity in this millennial world.

I conducted a poll to discover which characteristics are missing in leaders today that prevent them from being exuberant.

The poll asked, "Which attribute, according to you, is missing in leaders these days, that could make them exuberant?" The options were:

- A happy-go-lucky leader
- An articulate leader
- A dapper leader
- All the above

The results were intriguing: 43% of respondents felt that leaders lacked all these characteristics, 29% believed that happy-go-lucky leaders were missing, 19% thought articulate leaders were scarce, and 10% voted that dapper leaders were in short supply.

CHAPTER 6

STRATEGIC EXECUTION SKILLS IN A LEADER; A PRIORITY

Have you come across leaders who are caring, fun to be with, and energetic, but lacking in their ability to strategize and provide directions to run their functions or businesses? They usually shy away from making decisions and would not bother setting goals for their teams or communicating the set goals. Such leaders do exist and are often not effective at work. So, it is not just empathy or exuberance that matters for a leader's success, strategic execution is also a priority.

What is the point of an amazing strategy without the right execution? Similarly, there is no point in execution without the right strategy. Hence strategic execution becomes an inevitable skill in every leader. There is always a strategic leader behind every successful venture or initiative.

An effective leader derives or builds strategies from building blocks such as exceptional people practices, futuristic technologies, innovative ideas, and cross-industry experiences.

The attributes required for a leader to be good at Strategic Execution are **Strategic and Critical Thinking, Decision Making Skills, Business Acumen,** and an **Innovative mindset.**

Strategic and Critical Thinking

Strategic Thinking

Leaders are defined by the decisions they make and the execution of their strategic plans. Effective execution stems from sound decisions, which in turn are based on well-crafted strategies. These strategies are developed through strategic and critical thinking.

Strategic thinking is a process where leaders identify long-term goals, analyze their current situation, and determine the best course of action to achieve those goals. It involves considering diverse options and outcomes, assessing the risks and benefits of each, and making informed decisions based on the data and analysis.

The lack of strategic thinking can make leaders complacent, failing to challenge the status quo and being satisfied with their current operations.

How often do leaders in organizations communicate their vision and strategies to the larger audience? The CEOs, CFOs and all other CXOs should communicate their strategies at least once in a quarter during town hall meetings or through any other forums or mediums. Strategies are ideally drawn from the common vision of the organization. Managers and team leads can then derive goals based on those strategies and cascade them down to all the employees of the organization.

It is important to repeatedly communicate the goals and strategies to team members, so that they would not lose track of their goals.

Critical Thinking

Critical thinking is both an analytical and a reflective process. Strategic leaders use critical thinking to evaluate information, arguments, and evidence, to determine the validity of the communications they encounter.

A leader who is a critical thinker, would,

- Be open to all suggestions and ideas and pick the best out of them.
- Logically reason and support, with data and observation, to manage the performance of every individual in the team.

A leader who is a non-critical thinker would,

- Be strongly opinionated and often discount and discourage ideas and suggestions from team members.
- Fall for flattery from team members and provide them with differential treatment.
- Have favourites in their teams based on biases that could arise out of religion, region, culture, or physical appearance.

By combining strategic thinking and critical thinking, leaders can make well-informed decisions that align with their organization's goals and objectives. Both skills are essential for an effective leadership and decision-making process, and they require the ability to think creatively, critically, and logically.

Decision-making Skills

How decisive are the leaders these days?

Decision-making skills refer to the ability to effectively evaluate options and to choose the best course of action, based on a given situation. This involves processes, including problem identification, gathering information, generating, and evaluating alternatives, making choices, and implementing the decision. Effective decision-making requires good judgment, critical thinking, and persuasive communication and interpersonal skills.

Developing good decision-making skills can improve the leaders' personal and professional life by allowing them to make informed choices and achieve their goals.

We have all encountered leaders who struggle with decisiveness, especially those who fear making decisions. Sometimes, even senior team members who lack empowerment may turn to their leaders for simple operational decisions. These leaders often delay decision-making, leaving their team members to bear the consequences of non-performance.

Business Acumen

A leader in any function within an organization needs business acumen to effectively understand and manage various aspects of the business, including finance, operations, marketing, and human resources. This involves a deep understanding of the industry, the competitive landscape, and the key factors driving success, as well as the ability to make informed decisions that positively affect the bottom line.

Business acumen is crucial for leaders at every level of an organization, as it enables them to make decisions that are both financially sound and aligned with the overall mission and goals of the business. Building strong business acumen involves a blend of formal education, practical experience, and ongoing learning. Leaders with well-developed business acumen have a clear grasp of how their decisions affect the organization's financial performance and can make informed choices that drive growth and success.

Innovative Mindset

An innovative mindset is a way of thinking that emphasizes creativity, originality, and a willingness to challenge the status quo. It is characterized by an open-minded approach to problem-solving, a willingness to take calculated risks, and a focus on generating new and better solutions.

Leaders with an innovative mindset will always seek ways to improve processes, products, and services because they may not be happy with the status quo. Innovative leaders are curious and flexible, and they think creatively to generate wild ideas to find unique solutions to complex problems.

Leaders lacking an innovative mindset often:

- Avoid holding brainstorming sessions to generate fresh ideas.
- Fail to encourage their teams to take risks and learn from mistakes, and

- Do not allow experimentation or try new approaches.

An innovative mindset is essential in today's fast-paced business environment, where being able to adapt and respond to change quickly, is key to success. It also involves encouraging and fostering a culture of innovation within the organization, where employees feel comfortable sharing their ideas and taking risks.

You may be a leader with titles or no titles, an individual contributor, or a team leader, managing a small team or a large team; it is imperative to influence stakeholders, using these attributes, to be a strategic leader to implement great initiatives.

I conducted a poll to gauge the top characteristics of a strategic execution leader.

The poll asked, "According to your observation, for a leader to be good in strategic execution, which of these skills should they focus on?" The options provided were:

- Strategic and Critical Thinking
- Decision-making Skills
- Innovative Mindset
- Business Acumen

The results revealed that 32% of participants believed Strategic and Critical Thinking are the most important skills for leaders to focus on. This was followed by a tie, with 25% of people selecting Decision-making Skills and an Innovative Mindset as key to execution. Meanwhile, 18% of respondents favoured Business Acumen.

CHAPTER 7

THE ECUBE LEADERSHIP FRAMEWORK

In the previous three chapters, you read about **Empathy, Exuberance** and **Execution**, the three Es of effective leadership.

The product of these three Es is, E x E x E = E^3(ECube)

So, a leader who demonstrates the highest levels of Empathy, Exuberance, and Execution can be called an ECube Leader.

If we assess a leader's levels of Empathy, Exuberance, and Execution based on their behavioural traits and functional preferences, we can plot the results on a three-dimensional graph: Empathy on the X axis, Exuberance on the Y axis, and Execution on the Z axis. The leader's position would be within one of the eight cubes in the ECube framework, as shown in Figure 7.1 ECube Leadership Axes and Framework.

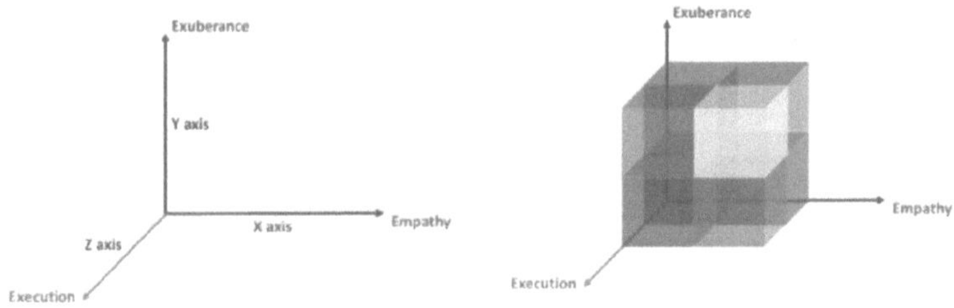

Figure 7.1 ECube Leadership Axes and Framework

Coloured Rooms for the ECube Leadership Framework

Red, blue, and green are known as primary colours because they correspond to the three main types of cone cells in the human eye, each sensitive to different wavelengths of light. This allows our eyes to blend these colours in various combinations to create the full spectrum of visible colours.

Different emotions are often linked to specific colours, such as red for anger and blue for sadness. Likewise, if we assign a unique colour to each attribute of the ECube Leadership framework, it becomes easier to visually represent various leadership styles based on their combinations.

Based on an intuitive sense, each attribute was assigned a specific colour: Empathy is represented by green, Exuberance by red, and Execution by blue.

In the ECube Leadership model, each of the cubes can be imagined as a distinct room, featuring a unique blend of ECube attribute colours. Additionally, it is possible to categorize and visually represent different leadership styles based on the combinations of these attribute levels as shown in Figure 10.1. The ECube Leadership Model.

This model offers to deep dive into the leaders' areas of strength and areas for improvement to help in their leadership journey.

The leadership journey involves acquiring and developing behaviours and skills that enable leaders to move horizontally and vertically between rooms, to reach the white room of the ECube leader.

How can we make the ECube framework useful?

In theory, the ECube Leadership framework provides an understanding of the three attributes and the various blends of these attributes. It would be intriguing to depict each leadership style as a uniquely coloured cubic room, stacked in a three-dimensional space, where individuals can identify their positions based on self-assessment.

To make this concept more practical, we need a tool to assess the levels of the ECube attributes in individuals. Varying levels of these attributes among individuals would result in different personalities and hence, different leadership styles.

CHAPTER 8

THE PURSUIT TOWARDS CREATING A PSYCHOMETRIC ASSESSMENT

Would it be wise to categorize all the leaders in an organization into the eight cubic rooms as per the ECube Leadership model, based on our gut feelings and estimations of their behaviours?

However, by understanding the ECube Leadership concept and a genuine self-assessment, individuals can estimate the specific "room" within the ECube framework that best represents their leadership style.

A psychometric tool that measures behaviours across the ECube attributes is essential for providing actionable insights.

To make the framework practical, a self-assessment must be developed first, followed by 180-degree and 360-degree assessments to evaluate empathy, exuberance, and execution skills in leaders.

Being an educator and a trainer by profession, I have used many psychometric tools, popular and unpopular ones, some validated, and some not, during my training programs. I also understood how these psychometric tools work and the principles on which they are built. They all follow a pattern in the way the questions are presented and in the way information is gathered.

It was an interesting activity to think and come up with as many questions as possible for the three attributes, Execution, Exuberance and Empathy. The list was exceedingly long for each of the attribute. A lot of time was spent analysing and selecting the most effective questions to include in the psychometric assessment.

Finally, I decided to have thirty-six questions for the ECube Leadership Assessment and to use a six pointer Likert scale.

It was puzzling and mind boggling to figure out the right way to grade the responses and arrive at a logic to get the best results. The next few months were spent experimenting with the tool to check on the reliability and validity of the test, an exercise I thoroughly enjoyed.

I have listed down all the questions which are a part of the ECube Leadership assessment. You may quickly browse the questions for ease of taking the assessment later.

ECube Leadership Questionnaire

Below is a list of statements about our behaviours in work settings. Read each statement carefully, and using the following scale, decide the extent to which it applies to you.

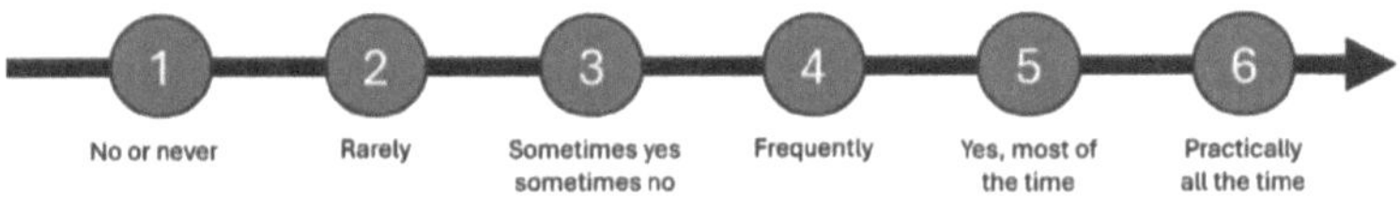

1. I prioritize compassion and relationships over logic in my decision-making process. My heart rules my head.
2. I thrive in the spotlight, grabbing any opportunity to be on stage to share my knowledge and experience through engaging presentations.
3. I find it difficult to consistently follow through on commitments and hold others accountable.
4. I create opportunities and allow team members to make mistakes for them to learn and improve.
5. I enthusiastically explore and generate ideas, whether they are good, bad, or wild.
6. I actively seek feedback from my team members/colleagues on my behaviour to make necessary improvements.
7. I often make decisions that prioritize collaboration and are reached through consensus.
8. I like to organize and participate in team-building events and trips that foster a sense of enjoyment.
9. I enjoy critically analyzing data and problems.
10. I am open to learning new skills and adapting to changing circumstances.

11. I prefer spontaneity over planned communication/ presentation.
12. I seek and respond to the individual needs and aspirations of my team members.
13. I openly address issues related to bias and discrimination within the team.
14. I encourage the team to have some fun at work and ensure a balance between work and enjoyment in the team's daily activities.
15. I prioritize logic and data-driven insights over compassion in my decision-making process. My head rules the heart.
16. I find it difficult to delegate tasks and responsibilities to my team members.
17. I exhibit enthusiasm even when faced with difficult or monotonous tasks.
18. I ensure that all team members are included and valued in decision-making processes.
19. I enjoy taking my team members for a break to chat and offer counsel, as I have a keen sensitivity to their needs and emotions.
20. I energize team members during meetings and discussions to keep them lively and engaging.
21. I prefer working with tools and processes rather than engaging with people.
22. I actively invest time in acquiring new knowledge and skills relevant to my role.
23. I communicate and engage with energy and enthusiasm, to inspire and captivate attention.

24. I proactively address conflicts and misunderstandings within the team by listening to both sides and having open discussions.
25. I prefer to get into every little detail and be in control of the team.
26. I find it hard to induce humour and lightheartedness to diffuse tense situations and create a positive atmosphere.
27. I review and evaluate progress objectively to ensure goals are being met.
28. I demonstrate a strong sense of ownership and responsibility.
29. I consistently find ways to inject positivity and excitement into team activities.
30. I actively listen to team members' concerns and viewpoints without interruption.
31. I struggle to manage my emotions and sometimes become very angry, particularly in challenging situations.
32. I am often the life of the party in work-related events.
33. I set clear goals and objectives for the team and follow through.
34. I like coaching my team members and guiding them to enhance their skills.
35. I dress for the occasion and like to project a powerful executive presence.
36. I make it a point to genuinely appreciate and recognize the contributions and efforts of every team member.

CHAPTER 9

THE ECUBE LEADERSHIP ASSESSMENT

Thank you for purchasing this book! As a valued reader, you are eligible for free access to the ECube Leadership Assessment*.

To receive your access code, send an email to **ecube@learningwiz.in** with your purchase and transaction details.

You will receive your code within two business days.

Once you receive the code, visit the website https://learningwiz.in

Navigate to the Psychometric tab in the top menu and click to open the Psychometric Assessments page.

Read the instructions provided in the ECube Leadership Assessment section.

---

* **Disclaimer:** The ECube Leadership Assessment has not been tested for validity and reliability. It is intended for learning, educational purposes, and personal development. Please use it as a tool for gaining insights and enhancing your leadership skills, rather than as a definitive measure of your abilities.

Enter the access code in the text box and click the Start button to begin the assessment.

You will then be directed to the first question with a 6-scale response format. Answer each question honestly and submit your responses. (Think of who you are right now and not what you want to be.)

Note that you will not be able to review questions once answered. Make sure to click "Submit" after completing all questions.

Wait for your assessment results to appear on the screen and take a screenshot if needed.

You will also receive a copy of the results via the email address you provided at the beginning of the assessment.

This report will include details about the ECube Leadership framework, your leadership style according to the framework, your strengths and personality traits, and highlight areas for improvement to enhance your effectiveness as a leader.

CHAPTER 10

ECUBE LEADERSHIP – RESULTS

The most effective way to understand yourself is through introspection. If you have taken the ECube Leadership assessment honestly, you can confidently trust the result and the report.

Like the Myers-Briggs Type Indicator (MBTI), where you have the onus to decide your personality type, you are the ultimate judge of your leadership style in the ECube Leadership assessment. The assessment serves as an estimate tool to assist in making that judgment. You have the final authority to override the reported type, as you know yourself better than anyone else.

Your scores in each ECube attribute will help you identify which ECube room you belong to, offering deeper insight into your leadership style.

Imagine plotting your position along three axes in a three-dimensional space: Empathy (X axis), Exuberance (Y axis), and Execution (Z axis). Your integration point will lie within one of the cubes. As depicted in Figure 10.1, the ECube Leadership

Model features eight cubes, stacked with four in the bottom and four on top. Your position corresponds to one of these cubes, each representing a unique "coloured room" that represents a specific type of leader.

It will offer valuable insights into your leadership style and the various types of leaders we encounter. If your peers/team members take this assessment, it will provide a deeper understanding of their leadership approaches and development journeys.

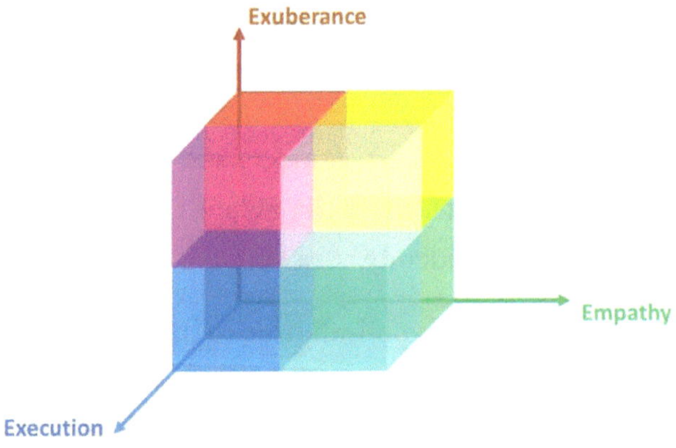

Figure 10.1 ECube Leadership Model

Titled Leaders: In the ECube Leadership framework, when leaders demonstrate low levels of Empathy, Exuberance and Execution (<= 60%) their leadership style tends to align towards the type called Titled leaders. They belong to the grey room at the corner touching all three axes as shown in Figure 10.2 Titled Leaders.

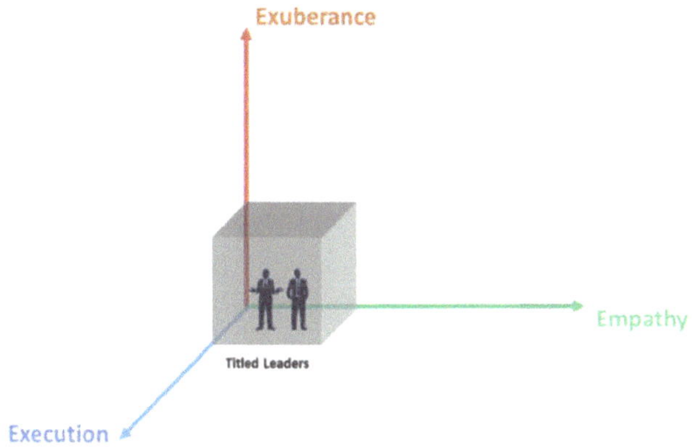

Figure 10.2 Titled Leaders

Empathetic Leaders: In the ECube Leadership framework, when leaders demonstrate high levels of Empathy (>= 60%) and low levels of Exuberance and Execution (<= 60%) their leadership style tends to align towards the type called Empathetic leaders. The empathetic leaders belong to the green room along the Empathy axis as shown in Figure 10.3 Empathetic Leaders.

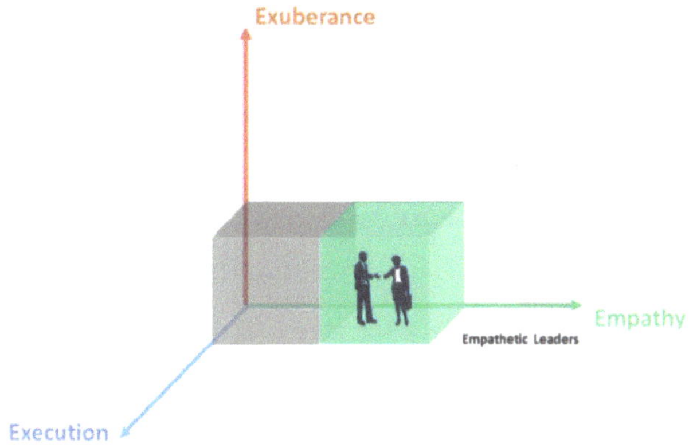

Figure 10.3 Empathetic Leaders

Exuberant Leaders: In the ECube Leadership framework, when leaders demonstrate high levels of Exuberance (>= 60%) and low levels of Empathy and Execution (<= 60%), their leadership style tends to align towards the type called Exuberant Leaders. They reside in the red room stacked on top of the grey room as shown in Figure 10.4 Exuberant Leaders.

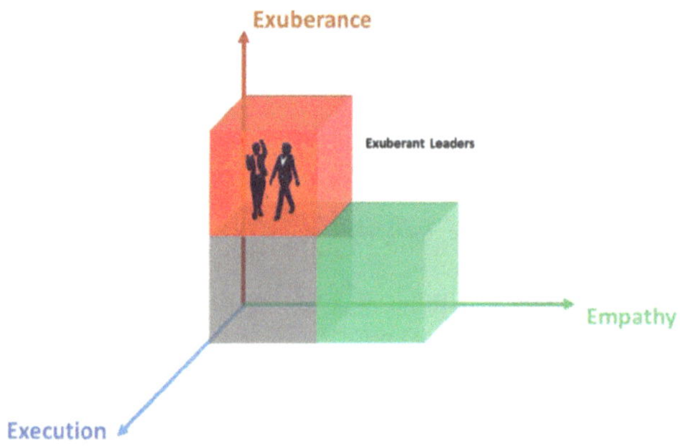

Figure 10.4 Exuberant Leaders

Execution Leaders: In the ECube Leadership framework, when leaders demonstrate high levels of Execution (>= 60%) and low levels of Empathy and Exuberance (<= 60%), their leadership style tends to align towards the type called Execution leaders. They belong to the blue room of Execution Leaders along the Z axis as shown in Figure 10.5 Execution Leaders.

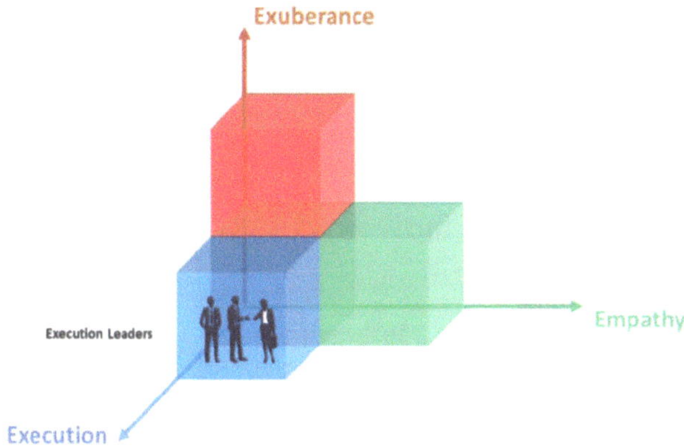

Figure 10.5 Execution Leaders

The Next Level Leaders

When leaders exhibit only one attribute at higher levels in the ECube framework, they may not come across as effective leaders. When they personify a combination of two or three attributes, they become more powerful as a leader. The style of leadership varies depending on the levels of these attributes and their combinations.

Result-Oriented & Visionary Leaders

In the ECube Leadership Assessment, when a leader demonstrates high levels of Exuberance and Execution and low levels of Empathy, then their leadership style tends to align with the Result-Oriented or the Visionary type. When we combine the red and blue colours we get purple, so the blend of the red room of Exuberance and blue room of Execution gives the purple room where the Result-Oriented and Visionary leaders reside. (Figure 10.6 Result-Oriented and Visionary Leaders)

The purple room, which is a combination of Exuberance and Execution will have leaders who would talk the talk and walk the walk. They do not lose focus on achieving their goals.

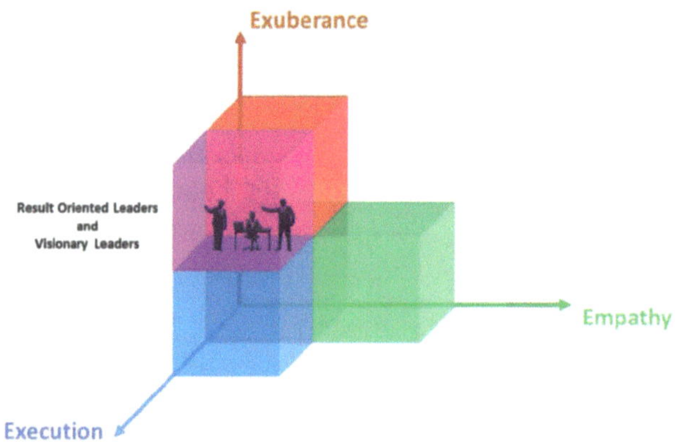

Figure 10.6 Result-Oriented and Visionary Leaders

Result-Oriented Leaders: In the ECube Leadership framework, when leaders exhibit high levels of Execution and Exuberance (>= 60%), where Execution is much higher (>= 80%), and low levels of Empathy (<= 60%), their leadership style tends to align towards the type called Result-Oriented leaders. They reside in the long purple room of Result-Oriented Leaders as shown in Figure 10.7 Result-Oriented Leaders.

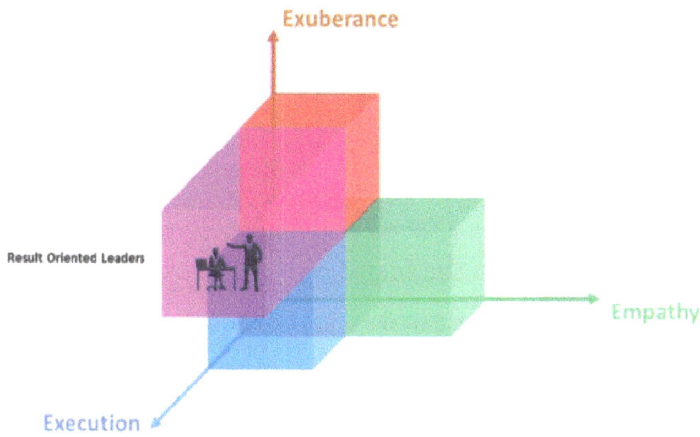

Figure 10.7 Result-Oriented Leaders

Visionary Leaders: In the ECube Leadership framework, when leaders exhibit high levels of Execution and Exuberance (>= 60%), where Exuberance (>= 80%) is much higher, and low levels of Empathy (<= 60%), their leadership style tends to align towards the type called Visionary leaders. They would belong to the tall purple room of Visionary leaders as shown in Figure 10.8 Visionary Leaders.

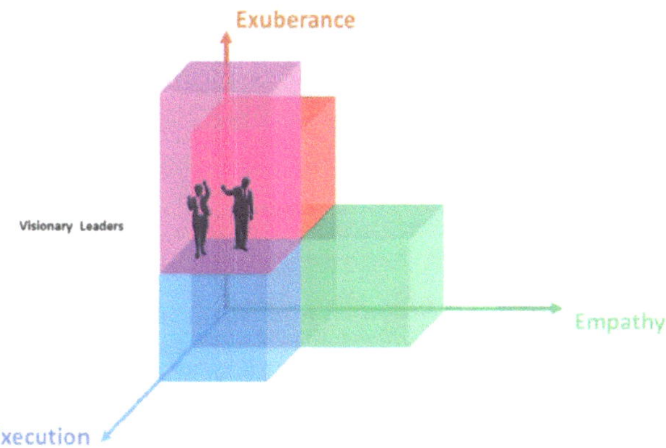

Figure 10.8 Visionary Leaders

Steward and Strategic Leaders

In the ECube Leadership Assessment, when a leader demonstrates high levels of Empathy and Execution but lower levels of Exuberance, their leadership style tends to align with either the Strategic or the Steward type. When we combine green and blue colours we get cyan, so the blend of the blue room of Execution and the green room of Empathy gives the cyan room where the Steward and Strategic leaders reside. (Figure 10.9 Steward and Strategic Leaders)

It is interesting to note that the cyan room, representing the combination of Empathy and Execution, produces leaders who are grounded, assertive, and may be modest achievers. While they may not always talk the talk, they consistently walk the walk.

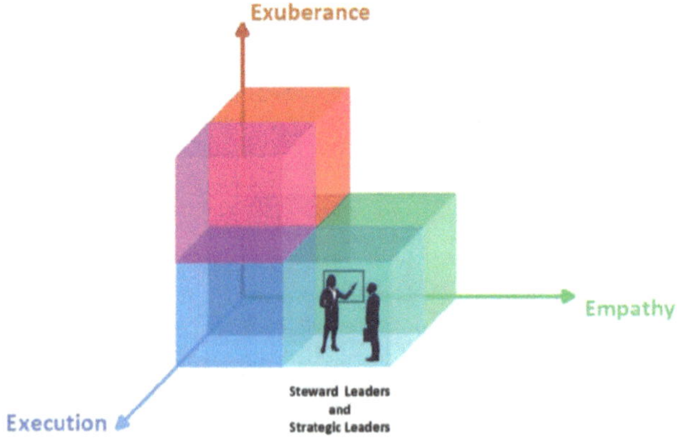

Figure 10.9 Steward and Strategic Leaders

Steward Leaders: In the ECube Leadership framework, when leaders exhibit high levels of Empathy and Execution (>= 60%), where Empathy is much higher (>= 80%), and low levels of

Exuberance (<= 60%), their leadership style tends to align towards the type called Steward Leaders. Such type of leaders belongs to the long cyan room as shown in Figure 10.10 Steward Leaders.

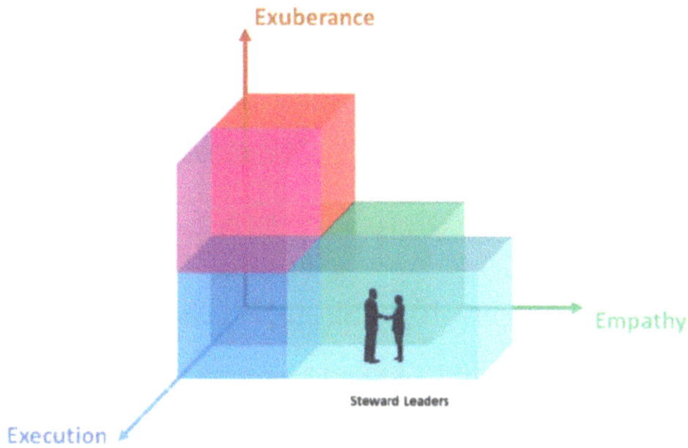

Figure 10.10 Steward Leaders

Strategic Leaders: In the ECube Leadership framework, when leaders exhibit high levels of Execution and Empathy (>= 60%), where Execution is much higher (>= 80%), and low levels of Exuberance (<= 60%), their leadership style tends to align towards the type called Strategic Leaders. They belong to the long Cyan room as shown in Figure 10.11 Strategic Leaders.

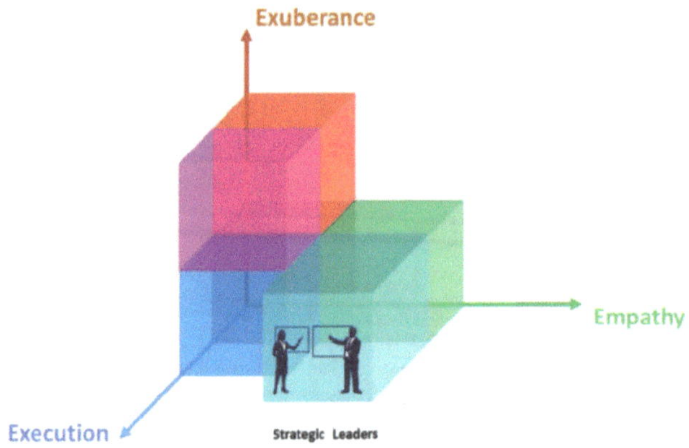

Figure 10.11 Strategic Leaders

People-Oriented and Charismatic Leaders

In the ECube Leadership Assessment, when leaders demonstrate high levels of Empathy and Exuberance and low levels of Execution, their leadership style tends to align with either the People-Oriented or the Charismatic type. When we combine green with red colour we get yellow, so the blend of the green room of Empathy and the red room of Exuberance gives the yellow room, where the People-Oriented and Charismatic leaders reside. (Figure 10.12 People-Oriented and Charismatic Leaders)

The Yellow Room combining Empathy and Exuberance provides leaders who believe in Inclusivity and can drive and motivate people. They may talk the talk but may not walk the walk.

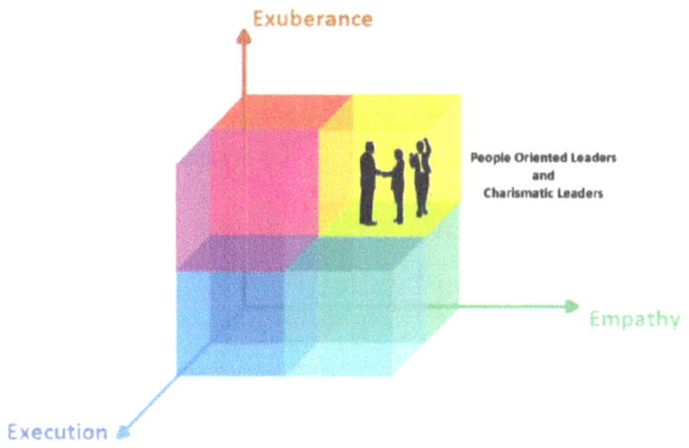

Figure 10.12 People-Oriented and Charismatic Leaders

People-Oriented Leaders: In the ECube Leadership framework, when leaders exhibit high levels of Empathy and Exuberance (>= 60%), where Empathy is much higher (>= 80%), and low levels of Execution (<= 60%), their leadership style tends to align towards the type called People-Oriented leaders. They belong to the long yellow room as shown in Figure 10.13 People-Oriented Leaders)

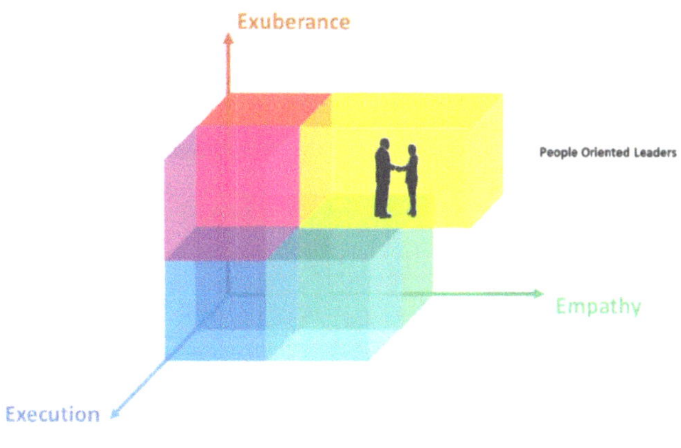

Figure 10.13 People-Oriented Leaders

Charismatic Leaders: In the ECube Leadership framework, when leaders exhibit high levels of Exuberance and Empathy (>= 60%), where Exuberance is much higher (>= 80%), and low levels of Execution (<= 60%), their leadership style tends to align towards the type of Charismatic Leaders. They belong to the tall yellow room as shown in Figure 10.14 Charismatic Leaders.

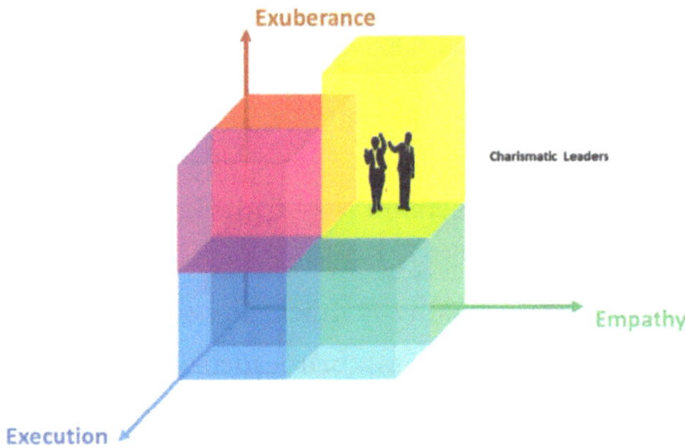

Figure 10.14 Charismatic Leaders

The Top-Level Leader – ECube Leader

In the ECube Leadership framework, when leaders exhibit high levels of Empathy, Execution and Exuberance (>= 60%) their leadership style tends to be ECube ready leaders and if it is >= 80% then their leadership style tends to align towards the type called ECube Leaders. They belong to the white room as shown in Figure 10.15 ECube Leaders.

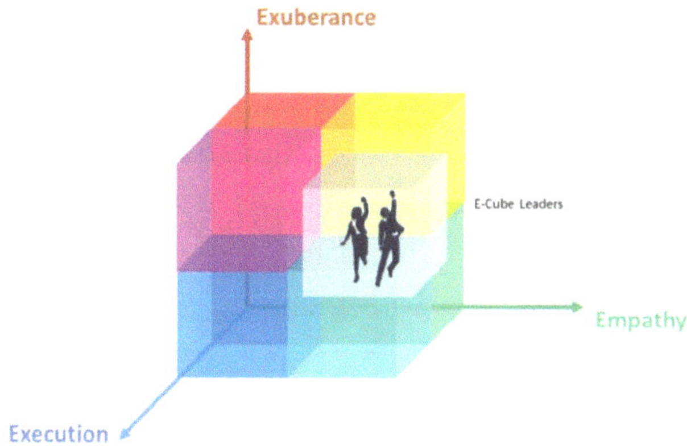

Figure 10.15 ECube Leaders

The need to adapt leadership styles based on different situations is crucial. Leaders must exit one coloured room and enter another, either vertically or horizontally, to flex their leadership approach. (e.g., from the blue room of Execution to the cyan room of Steward or Strategic Leaders when dealing with people) This allows them to practice various leadership styles and ultimately progress toward the white room of ECube Leaders.

The leadership styles outlined in the ECube Leadership framework extend beyond traditional dictionary definitions and any singular leadership concepts.

The following chapters will provide you with an overview of the different styles of leaders based on the ECube Leadership framework.

Leadership Style, Attribute Scores & Tendencies

Leadership Style	Room	Empathy	Exuberance	Execution
Titled Leader	Grey	<= 60%	<= 60%	<= 60%
Empathetic Leader	Green	**>= 60%**	<= 60%	<= 60%
Exuberant Leader	Red	<= 60%	**>= 60%**	<= 60%
Execution Leader	Blue	<= 60%	<= 60%	**>= 60%**
Result Oriented Leader	Purple – Long	<= 60%	**>= 60%**	**>= 80%**
Visionary Leader	Purple – Tall	<= 60%	**>= 80%**	**>= 60%**
Steward Leader	Cyan – Long	**>= 80%**	<= 60%	**>= 60%**
Strategic Leader	Cyan – Long	**>= 60%**	<= 60%	**>= 80%**
People Oriented Leader	Yellow – Long	**>= 80%**	**>= 60%**	<= 60%
Charismatic Leader	Yellow – Tall	**>= 60%**	**>= 80%**	<= 60%
ECube Ready Leader	White	**>= 60%**	**>= 60%**	**>= 60%**
ECube Leader	White – Standout	**>= 80%**	**>= 80%**	**>= 80%**

Table 10.1

Leadership Style	Tendencies
Titled Leader	Tends to be lazy, passive-aggressive, narcissistic and sarcastic – an insecure leader.
Empathetic Leader	Tends to be a good listener, adaptable, laid-back and aimless – an amiable person.
Exuberant Leader	Tends to be enthusiastic, fun-loving, seeking acceptance and impulsive decision makers – a motivator.
Execution Leader	Tends to organize tasks, make logical decisions, maintain a serious demeanour, and micromanage – a taskmaster.
Result Oriented Leader	Tends to approach deadlines with enthusiasm, make quick decisions, and take risks – an implementer.
Visionary Leader	Tends to infuse energy while brainstorming and articulating goals to get results – a storyteller.
Steward Leader	Tends to get consensus, provide support and compassion to meet objectives – a provider.
Strategic Leader	Tends to pioneer, balances logic and emotions, and delegate to achieve goals – a consultant.
People Oriented Leader	Tends to thrive in social settings, build relationships and networks – an influencer.
Charismatic Leader	Tends to exude confidence and charm, acts spontaneously, and seeks the spotlight – an entertainer.
ECube Ready Leader	Tends to balance Empathy, Execution and Exuberance.
ECube Leader	Tends to nurture individuals, foster harmony, and create an energetic, productive work environment – a coach, counsellor and mentor.

Table 10.2

CHAPTER 11

TITLED LEADERS

"When you were made a leader, you weren't given a crown, you were given the responsibility to bring out the best in others."

– Jack Welch

In the ECube Leadership framework, when leaders demonstrate low levels of Empathy, Exuberance and Execution, their leadership style tends to align towards the type called Titled leaders.

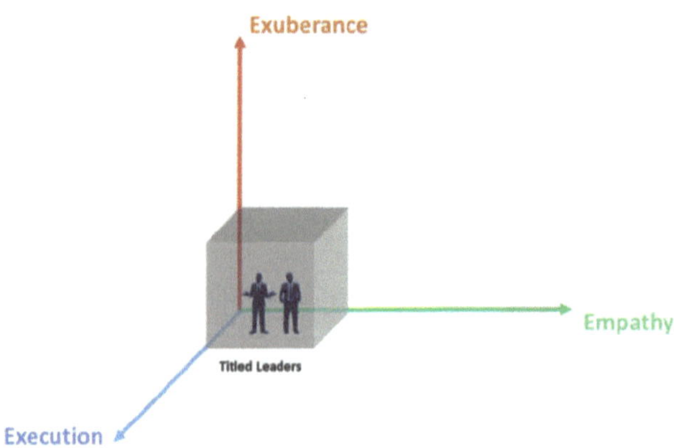

Titled leaders are individuals who occupy leadership roles solely based on their designations. They may have risen within an organization due to role maturity or tenure but often lack crucial leadership skills. In some instances, they might have attained these positions through ineffective recruitment processes. Such leaders usually stay in organizations that lack comprehensive methods for evaluating leadership potential and performance.

Have you ever worked with Titled Leaders in your current or past organizations?

It can be quite frustrating to work with such leaders. You would have noticed how the team members too share the same frustration when working under such leadership.

In the ECube framework, the grey room for Titled Leaders is situated in a deep corner, symbolizing how they are literally and figuratively cornered. These leaders are often unpopular among their colleagues. Their advancement within the organization is typically due to political, rather than genuine leadership skills or potential.

They must receive training and coaching to move out of this grey zone. Unsurprisingly, they often hesitate or even avoid self-development initiatives. Organizations need to address these leaders promptly, or they risk becoming liabilities.

Titled Leaders tend to be complacent and rarely challenge the status quo. They may exhibit passive or passive-aggressive behaviours, showing a lack of respect for themselves and others. This often results in sarcastic interactions or generally passive behaviour.

With low levels of empathy, exuberance, and execution, these leaders may struggle with compassion and people-centric approaches. They often appear unenthusiastic and lack focus on goals. Additionally, they tend to make minimal effort in acquiring and developing the skills or competencies needed to excel in their roles.

Team members often lack respect for these leaders due to their deficiency in leadership competencies, making them follow orders out of fear rather than genuine commitment.

These leaders aim to maintain the status quo within the organization, and look forward to retiring without making any meaningful improvements. They tend to drain the energy and resources of both the team and the organization, rather than striving for positive change.

Summary of Titled Leaders Style

ECube Levels: Empathy, Execution and Exuberance <= 60%

Colour & Type of the room: Grey

Characteristics: Submissive or passive-aggressive, lacking enthusiasm, and reluctant to question the status quo unless prompted by managers. They may be inarticulate, insecure, and hierarchical.

Priorities: To control people and to survive, self-growth over teams' growth.

Constraints: Not keen on learning and self-development, Non-communicative, dissociated, and uncooperative. May lack in clear professional and personal goals.

Fears: Losing Control

Dislikes: Being among competent and successful individuals, facing competition, and breaking hierarchy.

CHAPTER 12

EMPATHETIC LEADERS

"You want to be a great leader, start with empathy and change your perspective."

– Simon Sinek

In the ECube Leadership framework, when leaders demonstrate high levels of Empathy (> 60%) and low levels of Exuberance and Execution, their leadership style tends to align towards the type called Empathetic leaders.

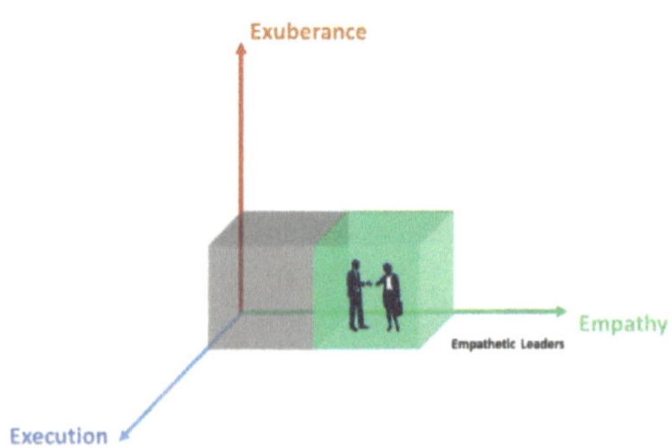

Empathetic leaders connect with the emotions, needs, and perspectives of their team members, customers, and stakeholders. They will create a supportive and compassionate work environment, fostering trust, collaboration, and employee well-being.

Empathetic leaders are good listeners. They respect the opinion of others and would not interrupt during conversations. Empathetic leaders are open to diverse viewpoints and are willing to consider different ideas and perspectives. They value diversity of thought and experience.

They grasp not only the words but also the underlying emotions and concerns of others. Empathetic leaders refrain from making quick judgments or assumptions, showing genuine care for their team and offering support when needed.

Empathetic leaders are adaptable and flexible in response to changing circumstances. They adjust their leadership style to meet the needs of their team and the organization.

They recognize the importance of work-life balance and encourage their team members to maintain a healthy equilibrium.

They take the time to build personal connections with team members, getting to know them as individuals and understanding their unique needs and aspirations.

Empathetic leaders create a positive and nurturing work environment, where team members feel valued, understood, and motivated to perform at their best. Their leadership style is associated with higher employee engagement, increased loyalty, and overall improved team dynamics.

Since Exuberance and Execution levels are low for Empathetic Leaders, they might sometimes come across as laid-back and aimless. They are people-oriented leaders but may not be result-oriented. Hence, they may find it difficult to set goals and push their team members to achieve them.

Summary of Empathetic Leaders Style

ECube Levels: Empathy >= 60%, Exuberance & Execution <= 60%

Colour & Type of the room: Green

Characteristics: Actively listen and make decisions with compassion and consensus. Communicate in a calm, non-animated manner and may come across as introverted.

Priorities: To foster collaboration and embrace inclusivity.

Constraints: May not push others to get results. Accommodative and passive, non-enthusiastic.

Fears: Losing trust, speaking to a large audience.

Dislikes: Disrespect and aggression.

CHAPTER 13

EXUBERANT LEADERS

"Exuberance in a leader is contagious."

In the ECube Leadership framework, when leaders demonstrate high levels of Exuberance (above 60%) and low levels of Empathy and Execution (below 60%), their leadership style tends to align towards the type called Exuberant Leaders.

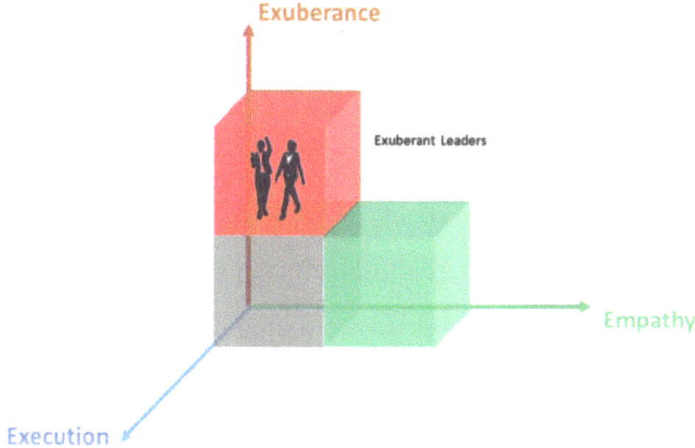

Exuberant leaders define their leadership style through enthusiasm, energy, and a positive attitude. They have a vibrant and infectious personality that inspires and motivates their team members.

Isn't it interesting to be around people who are energetic and joyful?

They lead, sell, and interact with exuberance, spreading their contagious energy and excitement, which helps foster a positive work environment.

Exuberant leaders are optimistic, and they spread joy around the organization and can boost the morale of the people by the way they interact. They are passionate about what they do and this often inspires team members and customers.

They are skilled communicators who can convey their enthusiasm and vision effectively. They use persuasive language and storytelling to inspire others. Their exuberance helps in exploring new opportunities and venture into uncharted territories. Their adventurous spirit may lead to exciting breakthroughs.

Exuberant leaders are resilient in the face of setbacks and challenges. They bounce back quickly and maintain their positive attitude. They like change and are open to new ideas and may be willing to take risks.

Exuberant leaders often have a compelling vision for the future. Their vision inspires others and provides a sense of purpose and direction.

Exuberant leaders can create a dynamic and vibrant workplace where creativity, innovation, and productivity thrive. Their enthusiasm and positivity have a significant impact on team morale and overall organizational success. However, exuberant leaders must balance their enthusiasm with practicality, ensuring their energy is channelled towards achieving goals. They may also need to be cautious of impulsive decision-making, that can lead to jumping to conclusions.

Summary of Exuberant Leaders Style

ECube Levels: Exuberance >= 60%, Empathy and Execution <= 60%

Colour & Type of the room: Red

Characteristics: They communicate with enthusiasm, are captivating presenters, and are the life of the party. Their enthusiasm shines in all aspects of work, motivating the team to enjoy the process. Extroverted, naturally spontaneous and creative.

Priorities: Exccutive presence, Instilling energy in groups.

Constraints: Impulsive decision makers and may lack implementation skills. May come across as egoistic.

Fears: Rejection of ideas.

Dislikes: Boring environment.

CHAPTER 14

EXECUTION LEADERS

"The best leaders are masters of execution."

– Robin Sharma

In the ECube Leadership framework, when leaders demonstrate high levels of Execution and low levels of Empathy and Exuberance, their leadership style tends to align towards the type called Execution leaders.

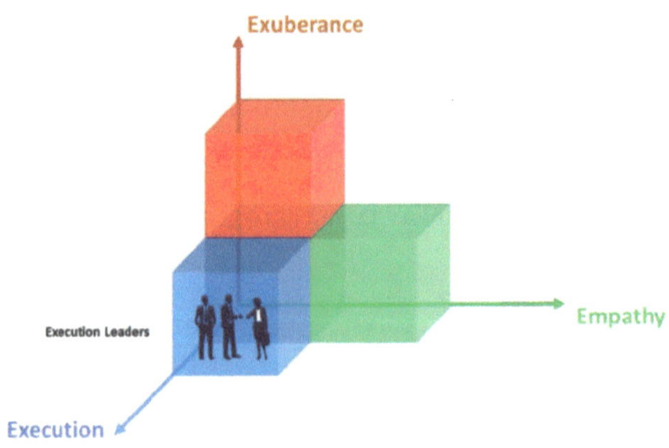

Execution leaders are known for their ability to effectively implement strategies, turn plans into action, and achieve tangible results. They drive results and possess a set of key characteristics that enable them to execute goals effectively.

They excel at planning and organizing tasks, projects, and resources to ensure efficient execution. They create detailed action plans with timelines and milestones.

Execution leaders are action-oriented and unsatisfied with just making plans.

They set clear, specific, and measurable goals for themselves and their teams. These goals provide a clear direction and serve as a basis for evaluating progress.

By holding themselves and their team members accountable for meeting goals and delivering results, Execution leaders establish a culture of personal responsibility within their teams.

Execution leaders make prompt and well-informed decisions. They are not afraid to make tough decisions and are willing to take calculated risks when necessary. They focus on efficiency and productivity.

These leaders rely on data and metrics to make informed decisions and continuously improve their execution strategies.

Summary of Executive Leaders Style

ECube Levels: Execution >= 60%, Exuberance and Empathy <= 60%

Colour & Type of the room: Blue

Characteristics: Skilled in strategy implementation, action-oriented, and decisive. They are risk-takers, practical, data-driven, and excel at planning and organization.

Priorities: To take action, to implement projects and manage resources.

Constraints: May tend to micro-manage, appear non-compassionate, and seem serious most of the time. Might not be perceived as fun-loving and may come across as insecure and aggressive.

Fears: Managing the emotions of others and addressing large gatherings.

Dislikes: Non-practical ideas.

CHAPTER 15

RESULT-ORIENTED LEADERS

"Result-oriented leaders are driven by action and they set and achieve goals with enthusiasm."

In the ECube Leadership framework, when leaders exhibit high levels of Execution and Exuberance, where Execution is much higher, with low levels of Empathy, their leadership style tends to align towards the type called Result-Oriented leaders.

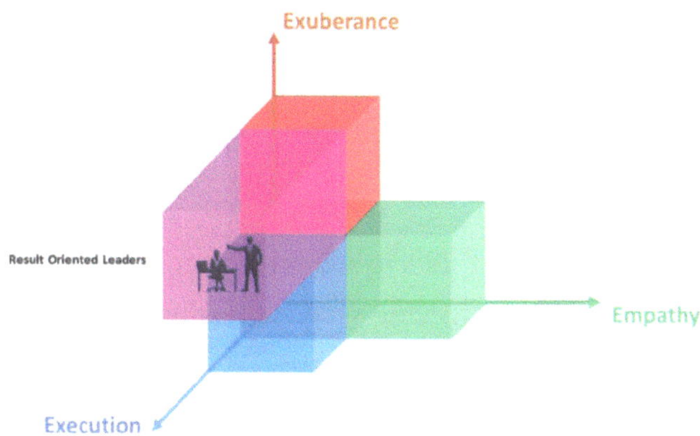

Result-oriented leaders focus on achieving tangible outcomes and driving performance by harnessing their enthusiasm within their teams and organizations. They are passionate about setting goals, tracking progress, and delivering measurable results.

These leaders hold their team accountable for achieving goals and emphasize personal responsibility for performance.

Result-oriented leaders make swift, confident decisions, avoiding indecisiveness and analysis paralysis. While they focus on achieving outcomes, they also understand the need for adaptability and are willing to adjust strategies with reference to organizational and environmental dynamics. They strike a balance between risk and reward, making tough, sometimes unpopular decisions that align with the organization's overall strategy.

They are good at motivating their teams to meet and surpass goals, creating a sense of purpose and enthusiasm for achieving results.

In addition, result-oriented leaders promote a culture of continuous improvement, consistently seeking ways to optimize processes and boost performance. They excel in managing resources—such as budgets, technology, and logical insights—to maximize the impact on outcomes.

Overall, result-oriented leaders are effective in driving progress, meeting targets, and achieving success, playing a crucial role in reaching objectives.

Summary of Result-Oriented Leaders Style

ECube Levels: Execution >= 80% and Exuberance >= 60%, Empathy <= 60%

Colour & Type of the room: Long Purple

Characteristics: Motivates and energizes people to meet deadlines and execute tasks, is action-oriented, willing to take calculated risks, able to make swift decisions, and adept at managing change. The end justifies the means.

Priorities: Setting clear goals, regularly reviewing progress, and ensuring consistent follow-through. Execute efficiently to achieve desired outcomes, with an ongoing focus on continuous improvement.

Constraints: They may seem non-compassionate and aggressive at times, focusing more on outcomes than on people.

Fears: Not getting the right results.

Dislikes: Idleness, passivity, feelings of helplessness and underperforming team members.

CHAPTER 16

VISIONARY LEADERS

"Without strong visionary leadership, no strategy will be executed effectively."

– Robert S Kaplan

In the ECube Leadership framework, when leaders exhibit high levels of Execution and Exuberance, where Exuberance is much higher, with low levels of Empathy, their leadership style tends to align towards the type called Visionary leaders.

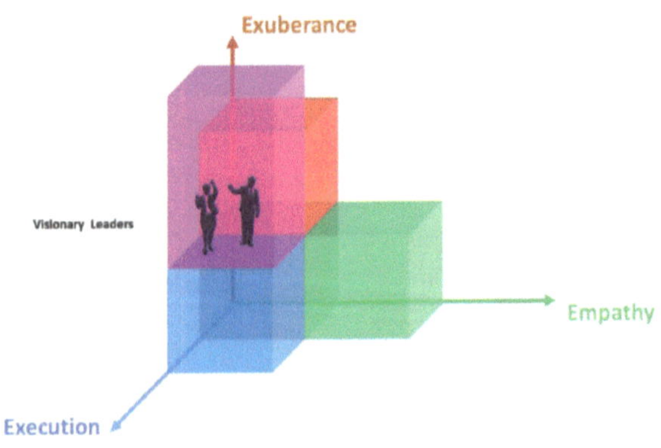

Visionary leaders possess a unique set of characteristics and qualities that enable them to inspire and guide their teams and organizations toward a compelling and future-oriented vision. They can articulate this vision in a way that inspires and motivates others to work towards it.

They are deeply passionate about their vision and can convey this passion to others. Their enthusiasm is contagious and motivates their team members to share in their excitement.

They drive innovation through energetic brainstorming sessions. They encourage creativity and are not afraid to challenge the status quo to achieve their vision.

Effective communication is a hallmark of visionary leaders. They can narrate inspiring stories about their success in project implementation and other successes. Visionary leaders may lack empathy but still, they can inspire and empower their team members to achieve greatness. They believe in the potential of their team and motivate them to strive for excellence.

Visionary leaders prioritize long-term goals. They can create a sense of purpose and direction within their organizations, motivating others to work toward a shared and inspiring future. Their vision serves as a source of inspiration and a catalyst for positive change.

Summary of Visionary Leaders Style

ECube Levels: Exuberance >= 80% and Execution >= 60%, Empathy <= 60%

Colour & Type of the room: Tall Purple

Characteristics: Enthusiastic, fun-loving, and communicates with energy to inspire others. Resilient and a catalyst for change, they are passionate about a shared vision.

Priorities: Impactful communication of vision and goals, expresses enthusiasm for new initiatives and drives change, and incorporates fun to boost productivity.

Constraints: They may lack compassion, act impulsively in their decision-making, struggle with active listening, and sometimes exhibit egoistic behaviour.

Fears: Not having a shared vision. Non-acceptance and rejection of ideas, goals and objectives.

Dislikes: Non-enthusiastic business presentations and dragging projects.

CHAPTER 17

STEWARD LEADERS

"The first and most important choice a leader makes is the choice to serve, without which one's capacity to lead is severely limited."

– Robert K Greenleaf

In the ECube Leadership framework, when leaders exhibit high levels of Empathy and Execution, where Empathy is much higher, with low levels of Exuberance, their leadership style tends to align towards the type called Steward leaders.

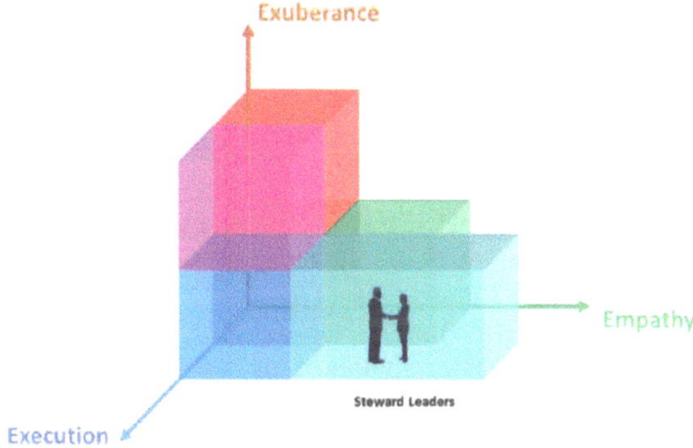

Steward leadership is a leadership philosophy that emphasizes the responsibility of leaders to act as stewards, or caretakers, of the organization and its resources. They view their role as providing service to the organization and its stakeholders. They prioritize the needs of others over their personal interests.

They make decisions based on the feelings of others and try hard to get consensus in meetings. They take responsibility for their decisions and actions, and they hold themselves accountable for the outcomes. They also encourage accountability among their team members. They provide regular feedback to their team members, highlighting areas for improvement and acknowledging successes. Steward leaders use constructive feedback to drive performance. They empower their teams by delegating authority and responsibility. They trust their team members to execute the strategic plans and provide them with the necessary resources and support.

Steward leaders consider the interests of all stakeholders, including employees, customers, shareholders, and the community, when making decisions. They seek to balance these interests.

Steward leaders develop their team members, allowing them to take ownership of their work and contribute to the organization's success. Steward leaders trust their team's abilities. They actively listen to the concerns and ideas of their team members and other stakeholders.

They value diverse perspectives and seek input from various sources. They foster a collaborative culture within the organization, encouraging teamwork and cooperation among employees and stakeholders.

Summary of Steward Leaders Style

ECube Levels: Empathy >= 80% and Execution >= 60%, Exuberance <= 60%

Colour & Type of the room: Long Cyan

Characteristics: They are compassionate, tend to listen empathetically while empowering their team members. Both assertive and approachable, they generously share credit and make decisions with a strong focus on people's emotions.

Priorities: Fostering relationships, offering emotional support to drive results. Focuses on well-being and getting consensus in meetings.

Constraints: They may sometimes be passive and not very outgoing and might struggle to make a strong impression in group settings.

Fears: Team failure.

Dislikes: Aggressive behaviour, enforcing ideas, and over-animated communication.

CHAPTER 18

STRATEGIC LEADERS

"Strategy without execution is hallucination."

– Thomas Edison

In the ECube Leadership framework, when leaders exhibit high levels of Execution and Empathy, where Execution is much higher, with low levels of Exuberance, their leadership style tends to align towards the type called Strategic leaders.

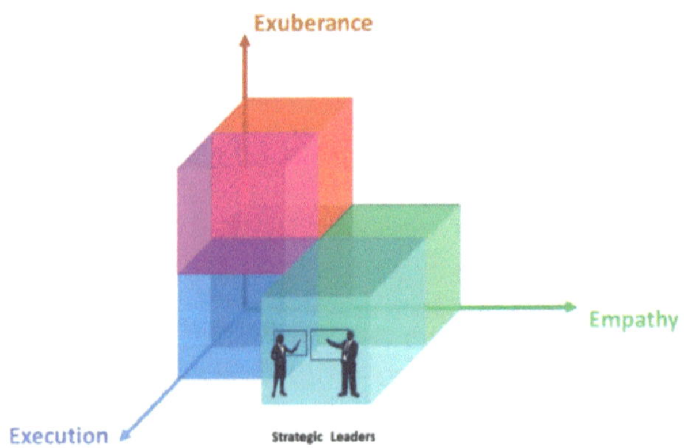

Strategic leadership is a style of leadership that focuses on long-term planning, vision, and the ability to guide an organization toward its strategic goals and objectives.

Since Strategic leadership is a combination of Execution and Empathy, they tend to be highly grounded and capable of spearheading numerous initiatives. They lay the groundwork for introducing new processes, products and technology in the organization.

Strategic leaders ensure alignment of the efforts of the team members with the overall strategy and goals of the organization. They prioritize long-term goals and strategies over short-term gains.

They ensure that everyone understands their role in achieving the organization's strategic objectives. They regularly track progress toward goals and objectives to measure success and identify areas for improvement for every team member.

Strategic leaders delegate tasks and responsibilities to the right individuals. They efficiently allocate and manage resources, including budgets, personnel, and technology.

Strategic leaders recognize the value of building relationships to achieve results and are prompt in establishing them when needed.

Strategic leadership is crucial for organizations that need to navigate complex and rapidly changing environments. Strategic leaders guide their organizations toward sustainable growth and competitive advantage by aligning their actions with a well-defined strategic direction.

Summary of Strategic Leaders Style

ECube Levels: Execution >= 80% and Empathy >= 60%, Exuberance <= 60%

Colour & Type of the room: Long Cyan

Characteristics: Critical thinker, decisions driven by outcomes, less talk and more work, excellent listener who ask insightful questions.

Priorities: Strategic planning with a focus on networking for results, achieving goals with minimal effort and managing performance.

Constraints: They may not prioritize fun and could struggle to energize their teams.

Fears: Unable to achieve strategic goals, project failure.

Dislikes: Inadequate project planning, dismal performance of self and team. Irrational arguments, and excessive verbosity.

CHAPTER 19

PEOPLE-ORIENTED LEADERS

"A boss has the title; the leader has the people."

– Simon Sinek

In the ECube Leadership framework, when leaders exhibit high levels of Empathy and Exuberance, where Empathy is much higher, with low levels of Execution, their leadership style tends to align towards the type called People-Oriented leaders.

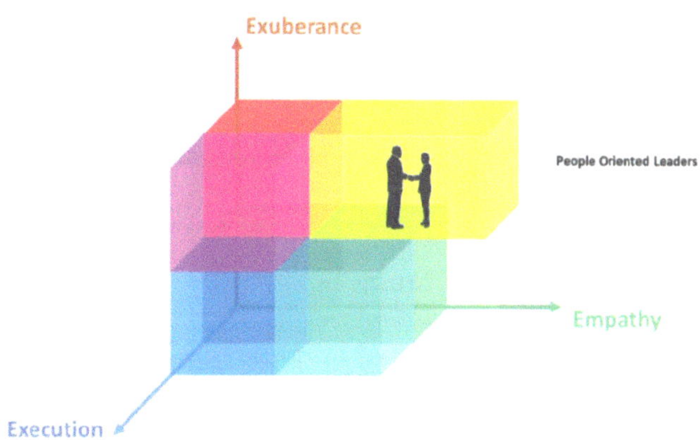

People-oriented leaders are enthusiastic about meeting people and being with people. They easily build networks because of their extroverted nature. They focus on building positive relationships, fostering collaboration, and creating a supportive work environment.

These leaders provide emotional support and encouragement to their team members. They help when needed and create an atmosphere where individuals feel comfortable seeking help.

Building a strong people network is a top priority for people-oriented leaders. They invest time in getting to know people in an organization on a personal level and foster a sense of camaraderie and trust.

They prioritize the physical and emotional well-being of their team members.

People-oriented leaders regularly acknowledge and appreciate the contributions of their team members. They celebrate achievements and provide positive feedback.

Summary of People-Oriented Leaders Style

ECube Levels: Empathy >= 80% and Exuberance >= 60%, Execution <= 60%

Colour & Type of the room: Long Yellow

Characteristics: They thrive in social settings, are extroverted, active listeners, and show recognition and appreciation for others. They are always approachable and follow an open-door policy.

Priorities: Develop a robust network of people, and cultivate a positive culture, balancing personal life and work.

Constraints: They might spend more effort on people and branding and might not get into action, losing focus on implementation.

Fears: Losing people-connect, non-acceptance from the team and audience.

Dislikes: Spending time alone, and non-engaging presentations.

CHAPTER 20

CHARISMATIC LEADERS

"Charismatic leadership is the ability to draw people in and captivate them with your vision and passion."

– John C. Maxwell

In the ECube Leadership framework, when leaders exhibit high levels of Exuberance and Empathy, where Exuberance is much higher, with low levels of Execution, their leadership style tends to align towards the type of Charismatic Leaders.

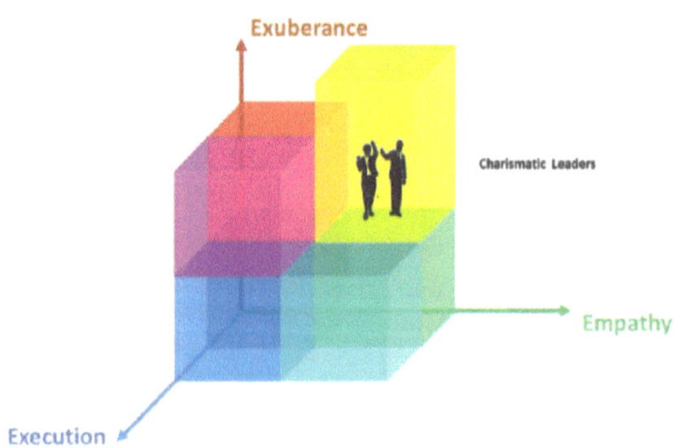

Charismatic leaders possess a unique set of characteristics and qualities that enable them to inspire and influence others effectively. They possess an executive presence that draws people to them and have a natural ability to engage and connect with others. These leaders can demonstrate high levels of enthusiasm, and spontaneity, and can think on their feet. They tend to empathize with individuals and and love to work in groups.

Charismatic leaders exude a magnetic and captivating presence. They have a certain charm, energy, and charisma that draw people toward them. They have high levels of self-confidence.

They are passionate about their beliefs and goals. This passion is contagious and can ignite enthusiasm in others.

They can adapt to changing circumstances and are open to new ideas and feedback. This flexibility helps them to stay relevant and effective.

They empower their followers by showing confidence in their abilities. This trust encourages followers to step up and contribute to the leader's vision.

Charismatic leaders inspire and motivate others to believe in themselves and the vision they are collectively working toward. They can share inspiring stories about themselves and other successful individuals.

They can be highly persuasive and can sway people's opinions and decisions through their charisma and communication skills.

Summary of Charismatic Leaders Style

ECube Levels: Exuberance >= 80% and Empathy >= 60%, Execution <= 60%

Colour & Type of the room: Tall Yellow

Characteristics: Extremely extroverted and enjoys influencing others. Fun-loving and energetic in social settings, often the life of the party. Deeply passionate about their beliefs and goals.

Priorities: Captivating the audience and seeking acceptance from others.

Constraints: In their efforts to impress others, they may lose focus on executing initiatives. They might lack attention to detail and struggle with follow-through.

Fears: No opportunity to engage with people.

Dislikes: Non-animated, non-enthusiastic discussions and interactions.

CHAPTER 21

ECUBE LEADERS

"I suppose leadership at one time meant muscles, but today it means getting along with people."

– Mohandas K Gandhi

In the ECube Leadership framework, when leaders exhibit high levels of Empathy, Execution and Exuberance, their leadership style tends to align towards the type called ECube leaders.

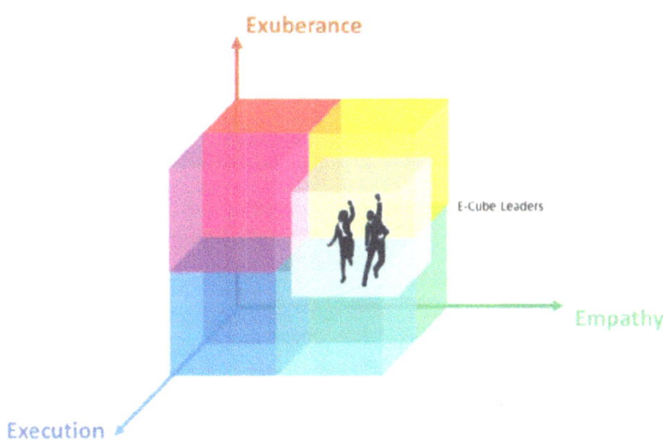

ECube leaders stand out from others by excelling in all leadership competencies. When you think of an ECube leader, you envision someone who could serve as a coach or mentor. They translate vision and strategy into reality. Their ability to drive action and deliver results is instrumental in an organization's success. They bridge the gap between planning and achievement, ensuring that goals are not only set but also accomplished.

ECube leaders motivate their teams to stay committed to the task at hand. They recognize and celebrate achievements along the way, boosting team morale.

An ECube leader aims to consistently develop people around them creating more leaders by coaching, mentoring and facilitating.

ECube leaders are adept at managing change within the organization. They can guide team members through transitions and help them embrace new strategies and initiatives.

ECube leaders excel at creating a positive workplace culture, boosting employee morale, and enhancing team satisfaction. They cultivate a sense of belonging and loyalty among team members, leading to better performance and collaboration.

Summary of ECube Leaders Style

ECube Levels: Empathy >= 80%, Execution >= 80% and Exuberance >= 80%

Colour & Type of the room: White

Characteristics: A continuous learner, extremely assertive and listens with empathy. They provide feedback, recognize and appreciate individuals, and are critical thinkers and excellent decision-makers. Emotionally intelligent, resilient, and enthusiastic. Can inspire and influence people.

Priorities: Coach and mentor to develop individuals, collaborate and innovate, turn strategies into realities and manage performance effectively.

ECube leaders recognize their constraints and swiftly address them by learning and acquiring new skills and knowledge.

CHAPTER 22

ECUBE FRAMEWORK – CONCLUSION

The Venn diagram below visually depicts the distribution of various leadership types within the ECube framework. ECube leaders are rare and hard to find in organizations, institutions, or governments. If everyone were to take the ECube Assessment honestly, we could accurately determine the population of each leadership style.

As mentioned in one of the earlier chapters, you are the best judge of yourself. You know which coloured room you reside in as per the ECube leadership framework.

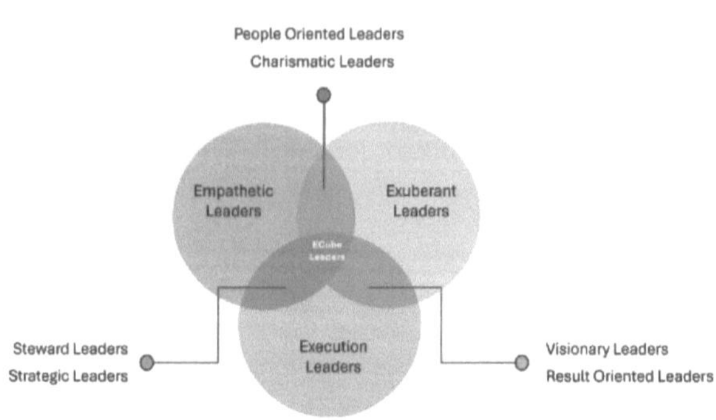

You could be any of the leader types mentioned in the ECube leadership framework. The objective is to advance from the Origin point of the three-dimensional space by enhancing your levels of Empathy, Execution and Exuberance and move towards the white room of ECube leaders.

We all have significant potential for growth.

Diversity is beneficial, as organizations need all types of leaders – except the Titled leaders.

The objective of the ECube framework is to foster leadership development and help individuals in their personal and professional growth. By taking the ECube leadership assessment and reading this book, you will gain insight into your leadership style, its characteristics, priorities and constraints, to help improve skills in your leadership journey. The ECube Leadership framework can be very helpful for leadership coaches, trainers and facilitators to develop leadership training programs to deliver for their clients.

Additionally, I encourage the Human Resources, and the Learning and Development teams, to use this framework to build Leadership Development Programs and Managerial Development Programs (LDPs and MDPs) to develop future leaders in their organizations and institutions.

MY BLOGOSPHERE ON LEADERSHIP

These blogs offer a glimpse into the core attributes of the ECube leadership framework, delving into a range of topics on leadership and illustrating them with diverse examples.

BLOG 1

WHO IS A REAL LEADER?

Who is a real leader? A leader is the one who is known, not by position or titles, but by values. Our world is rapidly changing and so are the leaders' traits and behaviors. Values combined with skills are extremely critical when it comes to the competencies of a leader. Most of the framework on leadership focuses more on skills like strategizing, execution, influencing and business acumen, but not on personal values which are crucial.

Real leaders will consistently work on the following value integrated skills.

1. Being a **Genuine** Coach
2. Display **Unbiased** Empathy
3. Deliver **Impactful** Communication
4. Possess **Collaborative** Knowledge
5. Make **Socially Responsible** Decisions and
6. Execute **Diligently.**

A Genuine Coach is a leader, who gives his team the freedom to make mistakes and passionately believes that failures lead to learning. They allow individuals to be creative, which results in building an innovative culture within Organizations. This type of a leader has genuine interest in people development and they constantly keep looking for skills and behaviors that can be improved. You may have seen Organizations adopt innovative tools like Design Thinking and Co-creation, only because of these kinds of leaders.

Empathy must be unbiased. A leader who has this trait of **unbiased empathy** respects every individual and treats them with no divisive mindset. Recognizing emotions in others and communicating positively to bring harmony is what these leaders do. No one wants a bigot as a leader.

Would you accept somebody with average communication skills as a leader? A leader should have the ability to deliver **Impactful Communication** to motivate others. The term impactful not only means the leaders' oratorical skills but also skills in expressing values like integrity and transparency. Exhibiting positive personal values while communicating gives an impact as powerful as a successful take-off of a rocket.

All of us rely on the knowledge we gain through our experiences, and wisdom is the application of this knowledge at the right time. Competition is the extreme opposite of collaboration. Some people compete with others using their knowledge negatively, like showing off their expertise or putting people down. If one can collaborate by creating learning opportunities and sharing what they know, then this leader is a person with **collaborative knowledge**.

A real leader makes **socially responsible decisions** by understanding the impact of those decisions. How do these decisions affect people? It is a moral dilemma to decide what takes precedence, people, or the task. 'Situational Leadership' talks about this. It gives a canned approach for leaders to behave in a particular situation. Real leaders involve their team while making decisions to understand the impact that would be caused and proactively arrive at ways to mitigate the effect.

> *"What we ever hope to do with ease, we must first learn to do with diligence."*
>
> **– Samuel Johnson**

Diligent execution of strategies after carcful analysis of the probable impact on people is a habit that all leaders should inculcate. Persistence and conscientiousness are the two words that make a leader diligent. It is the conscious choice of a good leader, to recognize the impact of decisions and analyze events during the execution of these decisions.

BLOG 2

AN INSECURE LEADER; A DETRIMENT TO THE ORGANIZATION AND THE COUNTRY

Anxiety is at its peak for employees during the last quarter of the fiscal year as it is the time for evaluations, assessments, and performance appraisals. The sales team would be behind numbers and the delivery and operations team behind deadlines. Later during the first quarter, the annual appraisal gets initiated, and the employees become busy highlighting their achievements of the assessment year. Few get good ratings through diligence and genuine hard work. Some shrewd individuals get excellent ratings by being in their manager's good books either by flattery or by being extensively submissive.

If a manager is a humble and a confident leader, then all sincere team members get recognized and rewarded. On the contrary, if a manager is an insecure leader, it would be frustrating for performers and high potentials, as they may not be appreciated, leading to quiet quitting.

An insecure leader becomes detrimental to the team and the organization.

Performance appraisals are ideally not a scorecard of the past. It is the preparation for the future. A self-confident leader would coach their team members for the future whereas an insecure leader often blames their team members concerning the past. A confident leader spends quality time with their team members during appraisal reviews whereas an insecure leader does it over an e-mail with no face time.

The personality trait of an insecure leader

In the DiSC psychometric analysis, a person with a highly dominant personality trait often exhibits behaviours that come across as insecure and controlling. When an insecure leader manages a team, empowerment is stifled. They tend to discourage positive initiatives simply because the ideas did not originate from them or were not communicated beforehand. The mantra of such insecure leaders becomes, "Seek permission or face consequences."

There are two deadly combinations: an aggressive insecure leader, and a passive-aggressive insecure leader. Team members may struggle if their managers are one of these types. An aggressive insecure leader might lock horns with you directly whereas a passive-aggressive insecure leader will do all the damage, behind your back. They may not have the courage to face and confront conflicts.

Characteristics of an Insecure Leader

How would you identify an insecure leader?

Here are some of the characteristics of insecure leaders that can help you recognize them.

1. **Lack of Confidence**: An insecure leader is often hesitant and indecisive. They lack confidence in their abilities, leading to poor decision-making, indecision, and a lack of clarity in their communication.
2. **Lack of Empathy**: Insecure leaders fail to empathize with the struggles and concerns of their team members. They focus solely on their personal needs and goals, creating a toxic work environment leading to high turnover rates.
3. **Micro-Management:** Insecure leaders tend to micromanage their employees, which can create a toxic work environment. This behaviour reflects a lack of trust in the team's abilities and results in decreased morale and productivity.
4. **Resistance to Feedback**: Insecure leaders often find it difficult to accept critical feedback, which can cause them to become defensive or dismissive. This behavior can lead to communication breakdowns and erode trust between the leader and their team.
5. **Blaming Others**: Insecure leaders are quick to blame others for their mistakes or shortcomings. This behaviour can create a culture of fear and defensiveness, where team members are afraid to take risks or make mistakes.
6. **Need for Control**: Insecure leaders often feel the need to always be in control. They struggle to empower managers and delegate tasks or share responsibilities, and this can lead

to burnout and create a lack of growth opportunities for the team members.

Innovation suffers in the hands of an insecure leader

One of the guidelines for innovation is to ask for forgiveness and not permission. When you want to try out or experiment with something new, do it, and if it fails, ask for forgiveness. Permission to try out new things or to experiment, mostly ends with denial.

I have been fortunate to have had great managers throughout my career. One such manager from an earlier job pointed out that I had missed a couple of my achievements in my self-assessment form during an appraisal discussion. This moment highlighted how a leader should be genuinely dedicated to their team's development. I accepted him as a mentor and continue to value his experiences and advice to this day.

I also have dealt with managers who do not bother to coach or develop anybody in their team. Such insecure leaders are hated and forgotten.

It is your choice. Who do you want to be? A self-confident leader, the one who is liked by all or an insecure leader who would be despised by the high-potential and confident team members.

BLOG 3

AN INSECURE JOB; A CRISIS AT THE WORKPLACE

The feeling of insecurity in your job or role can be a huge crisis at the workplace. The mental wellness of the employee would be deeply affected by this crisis. How many of us go through this crisis in the corporate world?

Here are some of the reasons why one could become insecure in their job.

1. Low Skills: The feeling that one is not skilled enough may reduce one's confidence levels and may lead to an insecure feeling.
2. Redundant role: Automation and other advanced technology skills can make the role redundant or even obsolete.
3. Non-empathetic and Insecure Leaders: Most people leave their bosses, not their jobs. Many leave the non-conducive culture of the organization built by such leaders.
4. Low Financial Health of the Organization or Business Unit: When an organization or a business unit does not perform in

terms of top-line and bottom-line, it would affect the morale of employees which would lead to a crisis at the workplace.

5. Mid-life career crisis – Choosing a career which is not your genuine interest will lead to disengagement in work and may lead to a crisis at the workplace.

Low Skills and Redundant Roles are problems that are within our control. One can upskill or cross-skill themselves to resolve this problem. Continuous learning should become a habit for all employees to keep themselves abreast of the current trends. Quick learning has become a new normal. How quickly one can learn and apply new technologies is more favoured than somebody with super expertise in legacy technology skills.

Leaders have all the power to construct or destroy the morale of employees in an organization. Some leaders build camaraderie in teams and would bring people together to achieve results and then there are leaders who suck the energy out of people, micromanage, and make hurtful decisions to achieve goals at the expense of the team's morale.

How would you manage the problem of the latter, the **non-empathetic and insecure leaders,** being the reason for the insecure feelings of employees? Can you even think of reporting to a cruel boss, a problem which could be beyond your circle of influence? The employee will be helpless and may have to quickly look out for other options.

Spot an Idiot

While I was browsing through the various posts on LinkedIn, I came across a video titled, 'How do you spot an idiot?'

Mr. J B Pritzker, the governor of Illinois, is seen delivering this speech at a convocation ceremony at Northwestern University. The video was interesting as he clearly articulated his thoughts.

"If you want to spot an idiot, look for the person who is cruel."

"Cruelty is the means to gain power, but empathy and compassion are considered weak."

He closes his speech by saying. "The kindest person in the room is the smartest."

So how about the leaders we work with in Organizations; Are they kind or cruel?

Kind and empathetic leaders build cohesive teams, where the team members feel safe and secure in their jobs while cruel leaders make teams dysfunctional.

Can we say with certainty, that the feeling of insecurity – the crisis at the workplace, stems from leaders who are cruel and unkind?

Crisis Scenario

How would you handle a difficult manager or boss who lacks empathy; One who makes only unilateral decisions, shows favouritism, holds grudges, and is strongly opinionated, with little regard for the team's well-being?

BLOG 4

FAREWELLS AND FUNERALS

I sometimes feel that as human beings, we respect the dead more than the living. One of the customs in any religion is to use rituals and traditions to pay homage to the deceased. But for these rituals and traditions, I wonder how we would have treated the dead. I had been to many funeral services. I saw relatives and friends of the departed soul come forward to deliver the eulogy, to shower praises on the person who lay there inanimate, in the coffin. While those eulogies came with appreciation and good memories about the dead person, the chats and the murmurs also kept coming around:

"He was a good human being, and that's why God took him early."

"She is blessed that she had seen many generations before God took her."

"He was a drunkard but a god-fearing man."

"He was rude to his family but a gentleman to the outside world."

I sat there thinking, why now? Why were those good words not spoken earlier when the person was alive?

I like to draw a parallel here; something that happens in organizations during the farewell of an employee. I do not want to equate farewells to funerals. But you could see team members and friends come forward to share their experiences with this employee and shower praise and appreciation on their last day of work. Many would have felt, why were those good words not spoken earlier while the employee was with the Organization? If this person was so good, why wouldn't they retain this employee? Why is it that we appreciate and recognize people only during their last days in the Organization?

At work, how often do we unconditionally appreciate our team members? How many times have we said these to a fellow worker?

"You are a good person."

"I am happy that you are in my team."

"You are good with people and looks like they love being with you."

Not many times, is it not? We would usually appreciate or criticize the work done by the team members or their behaviour in certain situations. Most of us would have used phrases like:

"The report you made is great."

"I loved your presentation. You made us proud."

"You could have structured the report in a better way."

"I see you not collaborating with our team."

Providing positive or negative feedback on a task or behaviour is always recommended. However, unconditional appreciation or criticism directed towards a person is even more powerful and can build or break relationships.

Some leaders struggle to deliver negative feedback during appraisal discussions or when addressing interpersonal conflicts. They may shy away and not engage in those difficult conversations. This can lead to assumptions and negatively impact the communication of performance ratings to team members, resulting in dysfunctional teams. One of the reasons could be that leaders consider giving feedback as a one-time affair during the appraisal cycle. They do not realize that feedback and recognition should always be a continuous process running throughout the year. Nowadays, most HR management systems come with the Continuous Feedback feature to manage performance. To effectively use this feature, leaders should focus on training their managers to give feedback and the rest of the employees to receive feedback.

The onus is on the leaders to create an environment that helps in articulating transparent and open feedback within teams. Unconditional appreciation directed towards a team member, and positive or negative feedback on tasks and behaviours would help transform any workplace into a harmonious and performance-driven environment.

BLOG 5

A SKILL THE WORLD NEEDS FOR A BETTER TOMORROW

To be or not to be, to do or not to do, to blog or not to blog; It has been a dilemma for more than three years to write about this topic and post it as a blog. The matter may not be as serious as Hamlet's dilemma, whether to exist or not, but equally significant and sensitive, and hence the predicament. It is a critical skill, a subject studied and deliberated from 450 BC till today and has the power to change the entire world. Writer and poet Javed Akhtar, in the year 2020, received the Richard Dawkins International Award for being a practitioner and subject matter expert on this topic. I reckon you got it. Yes, I am talking about Critical Thinking, a skill that helps us reason out and establish what to believe and what not to. A skill required for all, especially the leaders of today.

Imagination and Communication

The evolution of language has helped sapiens to communicate and share their feelings with their fellow beings. The unique ability to imagine, along with the capability to communicate, has given man the power to influence other men. Since humans are the only creatures who can speak about things they have not seen, heard or experienced, they can make stories, spread lies, be sarcastic, cheat, complain and blame. They can also love, empathize, be compassionate, kind and polite. So, all of us need to acquire skills to understand intentions, analyze information and opinions, to make the right decisions and make these choices a part of our belief system. This process of filtering information, differentiating facts from opinions, validating data, and believing only when there is evidence is called Critical Thinking.

Critical thinking is the best defence against superstitions, rituals, traditions, and beliefs followed by many groups, cults, and religions. Do we blindly follow these practices simply because they were passed down by previous generations? A critical thinker would always question, evaluate, and verify these superstitions or rituals for their authenticity before accepting them into their belief system. Hence critical thinking plays a vital role in establishing the right set of belief systems in all of us.

Critical Thinking in Institutions and Organizations

The American Management Association (AMA), in the year 2010, surveyed employees of organizations to find out the critical skills required for the success of the workforce of the next generation. They reported Critical Thinking as one of the essential skills in addition to Communication, Collaboration and Creativity. Only a handful of Institutions and Organizations have started to include Critical Thinking skills in their learning catalogue to make their students and employees future ready. Since critical thinking helps us identify the right problem to solve and make effective decisions by questioning our existing belief system, this skill becomes imperative in all businesses.

Successful leaders make good decisions. Critical thinking is the most needed skill to arrive at impartial and informed decisions. Hence critical thinking becomes one of the core ingredients in leadership development. So, the onus is on educators in institutions and leaders in organizations to make Critical Thinking one of their core competencies in student and employee development.

A peek into the behaviour of Leaders and Managers.

In organizations, leaders usually rely on their existing knowledge to solve problems. They get conditioned to use a particular process or methodology that has given results in the past. One may notice leaders sometimes discount a new approach or an idea when they strongly believe in a tried and tested method or process. Innovative leaders value fresh ideas and insights, regardless of the employee's level within the organization.

Have you observed the following in your organization?

Do leaders discourage differences in opinions and disagreements voiced by employees in meetings?

Have you witnessed managers who favour employees that simply agree with them and act as 'Yes Boss' individuals?

Do you see leaders ostracizing employees who question their ideas and concepts during meetings?

Do team members remain silent in meetings, fearing the consequences of expressing disagreements or differing opinions?

If you have witnessed the above scenarios in your organization, it is evident that the leaders, managers, and team members need training in Critical Thinking.

Beliefs in Organizations

Many Small and Medium Enterprises (SMEs) and a few large organizations may bring their founder's religious faith and rituals into the day-to-day operations of the company. Employees belonging to these faiths may be happy, but others would feel uncomfortable and feel left out. Consider the following questions.

- *Should religious rituals and traditions be a part of business operations and employee engagement initiatives?*
- *Is it a good practice by organizations to give gifts, bonuses, or performance-linked pay to employees during religious festivals promoting a particular belief?*

I have worked in large organizations that do not allow religious festivals or rituals to be part of employee engagement activities. It may be a good idea if organizations can give gifts, and bonuses during non-religious events like Founder's Day, Independence Day, or Republic Day.

Critical thinking allows us to question traditions and rituals and eliminate unconscious biases, fostering collaboration and growth. Engagement activities should be secular, inclusive, and foster a collaborative culture within the organization.

Institutions should focus on Developing Critical Thinking Skills

There are many schools and colleges built on the foundation of religious beliefs. There is no doubt that these schools teach good values through their religious-based teachings, but would it help build a critical thinking society? Should students be counselled using religious views or purely psychological and barefoot counselling techniques when going through emotional turmoil? Religion is personal, and it should not become a part of any institution as it creates bias and discrimination in the minds of children.

Critical Thinking in our Society

The presence and application of critical thinking skills in citizens can build better societies. The varied beliefs based on caste, region and religion across individuals promote discord and disharmony, and politicians take advantage of this. Social media bombards us with information from all quarters. Do we take measures to ascertain the authenticity of this information before forwarding it to friends, groups, and families? It is the responsibility of every citizen to share information that is non-divisive, non-prejudicial, and authentic. Critical thinking helps remove biases towards an individual or a group and propagates sharing truthful information.

We will have a hopeful and progressive society if schools and colleges focus on developing critical thinking in students. A skill that can unite people where all individuals are citizens of the world, transcending all barriers with no discrimination; helping countries and societies flourish and be successful.

BLOG 6

THE PERSUASIVE POWER OF PROBING

The person who is questioning always takes control of a conversation.

Probing is the skill of asking important questions, which is essential in consulting, selling, negotiating, problem-solving and managing conflicts. All great solutions have emerged from asking quality questions at the right time. The persuasive power of probing consistently aids in problem-solving and making informed decisions.

What does the term probe mean?

- To open or examine wounds or other body parts using hands or a blunt instrument.
- A hand-held tool connected to a thermometer or other devices to measure any material's temperature or other attributes.
- Asking the right questions during an investigation to uncover the truth.

The word probe is derived from the Latin word 'probare' meaning 'to test' and in late Latin 'proba' which means proof.

To test or to prove a concept we need information. To learn and to know the required information, we need to ask the right questions. To ask the right questions we need to learn the art of probing.

Art of Probing

Effective probing is the key to positive outcomes in all our interactions. Consider the following questions:

- Would you like a job interviewer who sells the role but does not want to know about your skills?
- Would you prefer a doctor who provides treatment without asking any questions about your symptoms?
- Would you like a salesperson who boasts about their products and services and does not understand your needs?
- Would you prefer a counsellor who advises and does not investigate?
- Would you want to believe in something without clarifying or asking the right questions?
- Would you get the desired response in Generative AI without the right prompt?

It is obvious that the response to all the above questions would be negative, which tells us the prominence of probing as a skill.

If you have observed, I have asked too many questions in this blog. Well, questions help to engage with your audience. Astute questioning can foster divergent thinking, leading to creative ideas and innovation. A single question can alter the direction of your conversation, potentially leading to either a favourable or unfavourable outcome.

So, getting acquainted with probing skills is crucial across roles, at all levels. The good news is that we can develop probing skills through training and continuous practice.

Regardless of whether you are a corporate executive, doctor, engineer, lawyer, teacher or any other professional, undergoing training in probing skills can be beneficial.

Different types of questions

It would be helpful to understand the type of questions that would be appropriate to ask, based on the scenario and the purpose of interaction. While interviewing, it is better to ask Competency-based questions than Hypothetical questions. While consulting or selling, it is better to ask a few problem questions than a lot of situation questions. When coaching, ask more Divergent questions.

During an interview, ask more Competency-Based Questions.

If you are facing an irate customer, what will you do? (Hypothetical question)

In your current role, give me an instance where you have managed a difficult customer and what was the outcome? (Competency-Based Question)

While consulting or selling, ask more Problem Questions

How long have you been working on this project? What is the overall budget of this project? What does the future of your organization's digital landscape look like? (Situation Questions)

Do you find it difficult to reach out to your customers? Do you have challenges with the security of your digital infrastructure? (Problem Questions)

While coaching, ask more Divergent Questions

What is another way of looking at this? What are some of the possibilities for increasing our customer base? What different strategies can we use to resolve this issue? (Divergent Questions)

There are many types of questions; open questions, closed questions, high-gain questions, leading questions, evaluation questions, convergent questions and more. Getting to understand all these types of questions and their usage can help us structure our conversation better, to get the desired result.

It is important to practice asking questions wherever possible and observe the outcome of each question.

One can then script and document those questions that have given good results. Then eventually a database of questions can be built and referred to as a ready reckoner. It is the best ammunition that you can have for all your meetings.

Conclusion

Remember, questioning and listening are the two main pillars of consulting. Questioning supports and reinforces listening and vice versa. When you are solving problems for your customers, it would be advisable to lean on these two pillars for better results. Ask those good questions, listen for great answers, and then build your robust solutions. An effective leader should possess strong probing skills to handle conflicts, negotiate favorable deals, and resolve issues for their customers.

BLOG 7

LISTEN TO LEARN AND LEAD; SO, LEND YOUR EARS

"The art of conversation lies in listening."

– Malcolm Forbes

If someone asked you to choose your favourite person among the people you know, whom would you pick? The truth is you would choose a person who listens to you. You would like a person more because of the person's nature to lend their ears to listen. Good listeners make good friends. The skill of listening is key to learning and growing in your career. So, consciously learn to listen, and then you will be able to listen to learn.

The impact of listening

Listening reinforces and supports questioning. In my last blog, I wrote about the power of questioning and how it reinforces and supports listening. If you listen actively, you can learn from the person who is speaking. When you listen empathetically, you can understand the person emotionally and deeply. If you pretend to listen or ignore, then you will irritate the person who is talking to you. So, engaging people by listening will make them happy whereas ignoring would annoy them. Triggering positive or negative emotions in people depends on the way we listen.

Distractions, Virtuality, and Its Impact

In the present days of social media and smartphone distractions, getting people to listen and have a longer span of attention is a challenge. When you travel in a train, bus, or metro, and look around, you would see that over 95% of the passengers, sitting or standing would be staring at their mobile devices with their heads drooped down. Swiping and swiping through bottomless reels and social media pages. They do not engage in conversations, nor observe the real world, but are immersed in the virtual world. Perspectives are lost in this journey and our society is losing the skill of listening.

The immersive nature of these devices is killing the power of our senses. Among the five senses, hearing and sight are the ones we can consciously choose to use or not. We can close our eyes to block out what we see and intentionally ignore sounds around us. The other three senses, however are always used. We eat, and so we taste, we breathe, and so we smell, and we handle various things and hence the sense of touch. Instead of making our auditory and visual senses stronger, by observing and listening, in the present real world, we make them weaker day by day, being hooked to virtuality.

Respect & Listening

The best way to show respect to someone is by listening to them. How often do you observe people whom you speak to, who do not listen, but are more interested in sharing their views, or sometimes seen fiddling with things, or sneakily looking at their phones while they pretend to listen? It would be annoying to speak to someone like that. One would feel disrespected and ignored during such interactions.

Some individuals have closed minds and they rigidly adhere to their belief systems, convinced that their views are always correct while others are wrong. They may not be receptive to listening to different perspectives or explore alternative belief systems.

We can see that listening is the most important skill among the various other components of communication skills, such as reading, writing, speaking, and presenting. Listening as a skill is often overlooked in school curricula, whereas greater emphasis is placed on other language skills and technical skills. Some of the schools have language labs focussing on teaching listening skills. It is a welcome change, but only a handful of schools have the inclination, mindset, and funds to set up these language labs.

Types of Listening

There are several types of listening that we exhibit. They could include Fake Listening, Selective Listening, Active Listening, and Empathetic Listening, where the latter two are the ones in which we should engage.

Fake Listening is when someone is paying attention by nodding and maintaining eye contact but is disengaged. This often happens in dull environments, like classrooms, where students might use this tactic.

Selective Listening occurs when a person only listens to what they desire to hear and conveniently ignores other information. This happens during long speeches, seminars, and lectures. You also listen only when you like the speaker, or else ignore them. This is also a form of Selective Listening.

Active listening involves fully engaging with the speaker, understanding all the information being conveyed, and asking questions for clarification. This is considered effective listening. Good consultants actively listen to their customers to solve their problems.

Empathetic listening is the highest form of listening, involving not only hearing the words but also understanding the feelings behind them. This skill is not innate and must be developed through practice. Counsellors empathetically listen to individuals.

Conclusion

Good listeners strive to practice Active and Empathetic listening consistently. Listening to the aspirations, grievances, and pain points of your team members and customers will make you an effective leader. You may not be able to solve all their issues, but listening to them will provide emotional support and care.

BLOG 8

THE BRAIN, THE HEART, AND THE GUT

Life is all about creating options and making the right choices. The decisions made during a person's life are attributed to the individual's success or failure. A world-size canvas sometimes may not be enough to draw a decision tree with all the choices we had before us and the decisions made based on those choices, in our lifetime. How many times have we wished for a time machine to take us back in time, to change the decisions we have made?

When young, we are all dependent. It is our parents or elders who make critical decisions for us. We did not have a choice in these matters. As a part of growing up, we slowly learned the art of decision-making and started making decisions for ourselves.

Is decision-making art or science?

It is both an art as well as a science. We know that wisdom is the right decision we make, integrating the three elements, the brain, the heart, and the gut. It is merely symbolic, the heart portraying emotions and the gut being intuitive. Whether the decision is based on careful analysis or based on feelings or just a hunch; all of it is processed in our brain.

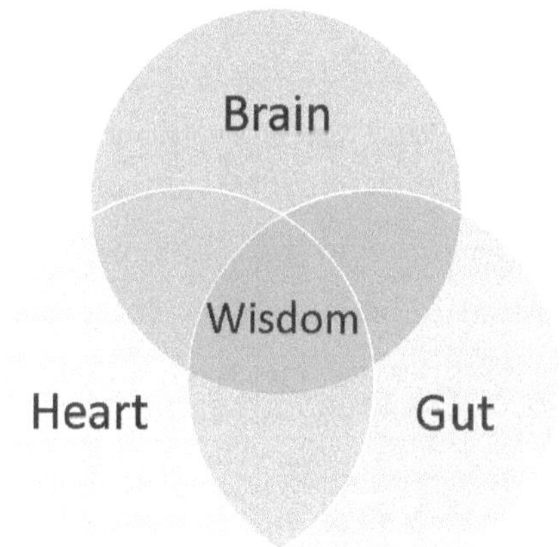

Figure B2 The Integration

> *"The intuitive mind is a sacred gift, and the rational mind is a faithful servant. We have created a society that honours the servant and has forgotten the gift."*
>
> **Albert Einstein**

Happiness, Sadness, Anger or Fear; which of these emotions do you think would help you in decision-making?

It is better not to make decisions when one is emotional.

How can one be emotionally neutral while making decisions? This can happen by being emotionally intelligent. The science of Emotional Intelligence is managing and regulating our emotions while making decisions and interacting with people. We often see political leaders using hate speeches to trigger anger and fear in voters, provoking them to elect their government. This demonstrates how emotions can be exploited to incite and manipulate people into making decisions that align with specific agendas.

Decisions Vs Destiny

What changes our lives? Is it the decisions we make or is it destiny? Ask a person who had bought shares after careful analysis, expecting it to be bullish and it turns out bearish. One can easily blame it on destiny. However, it is always decisions that can change our destiny.

Maximizing the number of right decisions made by leaders determines the organization's success. These decisions may be day-to-day operational decisions or long-term strategic decisions. The ability to make the right decision in critical situations is one of the measurable traits of leadership skills. The positive aspect is that we can acquire and enhance our decision-making skills. Leaders should learn on the job by evaluating past decisions and their outcomes. Ultimately, decisions define leadership.

BLOG 9

THE ONLY SKILL A LEADER NEEDS TO BE EFFECTIVE

The success of an organization depends on its leaders being change agents, thereby building leaders and effectively managing its people and projects. Are we not inspired by leaders who transform businesses, provide growth opportunities for people, impart hope, and achieve success for the organization and its employees? These leaders have the charisma and the right traits, and they are usually called the "leader material". It is continuous learning, preferably experiential, that helps leaders acquire these leadership traits.

In one of my earlier blogs titled 'Who is a real leader', I listed down a few value-driven skills as an absolute necessity to be a true leader. I received lots of feedback from my friends and colleagues, who agreed and disagreed with my theory mentioned in the blog. Well, blogs are not research papers; they are experiences and opinions articulated to derive certain conclusions.

The competency of managing change

A few years back, I read a book called "The Kite Runner" written by Khalid Hosseini. I recall a conversation from the book where Baba, the father of Amir, the protagonist, reasons that theft is the only sin in the world. All the other sins are a variation or a different form of theft. "When we kill a man, we are stealing life. We are robbing of a wife's right to a husband. We take his children's rights to their father. When we lie, we are stealing someone's right to the truth." It is purely the author's opinion, and I thought it was interesting.

Taking a cue from the 'theft being the only sin' example, I asked myself; what could be the single competency required to be a successful leader? After some serious deliberation, I found the answer to the question. It is Change Management. All the other sets of skills overlap and come under the umbrella of the Change Management competency. Leaders must acquire and develop competencies like Communication, Critical Thinking, Collaboration, Conflict Management, Creativity, Emotional Intelligence, Marketing Skills, and Decision Making to manage change effectively. The one who masters all these competencies will become an effective leader.

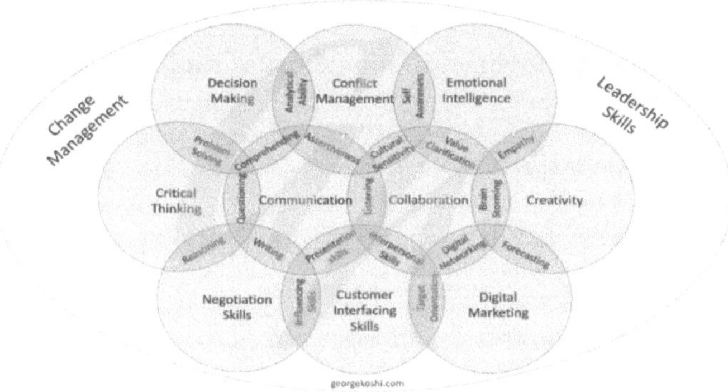

Figure B2 Change Management set of skills for Leadership.

Why do leaders fail to manage change?

Most of us agree that leaders evolve and rise to the occasion of change. Very often, it can test the leaders on various facets including behaviours and skills. Careful observation and analysis of a leader's behaviour while going through any organizational transformation will give us more insights into good and bad leadership traits. Some leaders falter, and some flourish during a change. Successful leaders engage in continuous learning, motivating, and influencing their teams during challenges while driving change. I have listed six deadly mistakes leaders commit that make managing key initiatives and transformations difficult.

The six deadly mistakes leaders commit

Mistake No 1. Not empowering managers.

Leaders should empower their managers to manage teams. When leaders bypass their managers and directly engage with the managers' teams to supervise tasks and initiatives, it can demoralize the managers and erode their authority, ultimately causing a loss of respect from the team. Too many review meetings and cadence calls will suffocate a team and may not help in achieving goals and objectives in the long term.

Sometimes even decisions made by managers on assigning jobs, allocating resources, and performance ratings of their team members are discounted and overlooked by few leaders. This micro-managing can cause a lot of friction in teams and be a cause for attrition among managers.

Mistake No 2. Not willing to communicate with junior employees.

Have you seen leaders who interact only with employees at their level and hesitate to speak to people below their hierarchy?

When junior employees approach these leaders for any interaction, even if related to work, the leader hesitates to speak and often asks for seniors to come over to discuss the same.

Mistake No. 3: Not providing learning opportunities for the team.

Change is perpetual in any organization. An organization that goes through these transformations will go through a Change Curve, reflecting the confidence and morale of employees based on adoption. Successful leaders take employees on a comfortable ride along the curve quickly. They should be instrumental in initiating learning drives relevant to the change for a smooth transition. The ride along the curve can become bumpy and uncomfortable when leaders do not provide learning opportunities for their teams. Moreover, giving timely feedback, constructive and critical, leads to learning opportunities, thus creating a performance-driven culture in the organization.

Mistake No. 4: Sweeping problems under the carpet.

Team members often bring problems to leaders, especially during major projects or critical organizational transformations. Leaders who acknowledge these issues, categorize them as either people or process-related, and take corrective action will excel and succeed. However, leaders who sweep these problems under the rug, particularly those concerning people, causes dissatisfaction among team members and harm the organization in the long run.

Mistake No. 5: Nurturing biases.

Conscious and unconscious biases in leaders are harmful to the growth of any organization. These unchecked biases can impact recruitment, promotions and even job allocations negatively. When leaders initiate and allocate resources for critical projects or key assignments, choosing team members they like based on gender, religion, region, or caste can discourage skilled and high-performing employees.

Mistake No. 6: Being aggressive or passive-aggressive.

Leaders who are autocratic, arrogant, non-empathetic or rude in their behaviour while managing or interacting with team members can impede the team's performance. Aggressive leaders do not respect others but only respect themselves. Even worse are the passive-aggressive leaders who flatter people on the face and speak ill behind their backs. They neither respect themselves nor others. Both these kinds of leaders are detrimental to the organization. When such leaders drive an organizational change, it could result in a disaster.

Conclusion

The team learns only from a learning leader.

A leader who continuously learns can rightly influence people. Their only objective must be to develop people by providing them with challenging opportunities and making them part of the change management process. This ensures that the team would acquire and develop all essential leadership skills necessary to drive success, foster collaboration, and adapt to the evolving challenges of the organization.

BLOG 10

FEAR AND FAILURE

Victory gives us immense pleasure. It is ingrained in our culture that winning is more important than anything else. Parents push and persuade their kids at school to be the number one in all their endeavours and win at any cost. Is there anything wrong with this approach? Well, a big yes.

Gerard Hendrik Hofstede, the Dutch psychologist, measured the masculinity index along with other cultural dimensions of various countries. Japan, the United States, and India have a higher masculinity index and this tells us how competition, achievement and success drive these societies. Sweden, on the other hand, has a low score, driven by the quality of life and passion for work. The fundamental difference is what motivates people, whether to be the best (Masculinity) or to like what they do (Feminity). The problem with the Masculine society is that we do not learn to cope with failures.

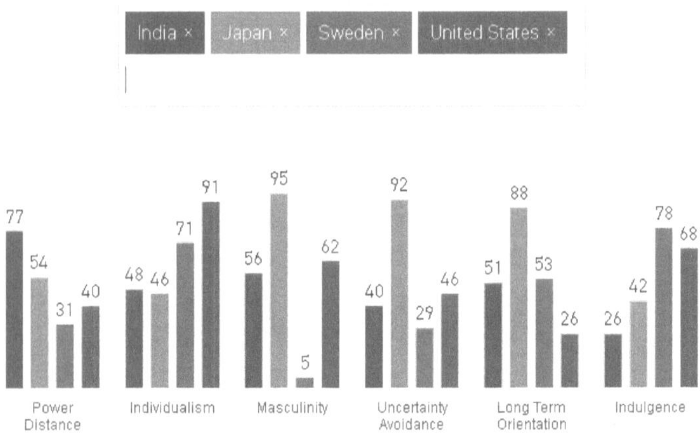

Figure B2 Hofstede Cultural Dimension

Here is an observation of mine while I was a part of the corporate Toastmasters club, where the members are registered employees from different functions. During the table topics session, members and guests are encouraged to talk impromptu on any given topic. I observed that while the millennials come forward to deliver their speech with no fear, senior managers hesitate. I opine that they do not want to fail, especially in front of their juniors. We all deter ourselves from saying and doing things, as we fear failure and fear the unknown.

The human being as a species has survived all these years. Thanks to the emotion called fear. It kept us safe and away from the dangers in the jungles we once inhabited. In the Corporate world, this emotion has become a deterrent to the growth of individuals. We all want to get it right the first time, leaving no space for trials and errors. Trying more often could mean more failures and, in the bargain, more learning, getting us closer to success.

We lean towards religion, astrology, superstitions, and ritualistic beliefs to cope with our fear of the unknown. Surprisingly, even the most educated believe in astrology, hoping that it can change their lives, often revering mythology as historical truth. Sadly, they use this belief system as a crutch to deal with problems rather than using their critical thinking ability.

"Fail early to succeed later."

Leaders of organizations should build a culture that encourages people to fail more often. Creating opportunities and building confidence among individuals to try and fail are the first steps in the innovation process. However, it is daunting for leaders in businesses, especially when they are pressed for time to deliver results with high profits. It would be helpful if individuals overcome their fear of failure by being passionate about work and start to like and enjoy what they do, instead of competing and wanting to win at every opportunity.

SUMMARY OF POSITIVE AND NEGATIVE LEADERSHIP QUALITIES

Positive Qualities of leaders

Characteristics of an Empathetic Leader

- *Uses the power of empathy and knowledge to develop people.*
- *Listens empathetically.*
- *Believes in collaboration over competition.*

Characteristics of an Exuberant Leader

- *An articulate leader: A leader who communicates with a lot of energy and passion.*
- *A happy-go-lucky leader: A fun-loving leader who encourages camaraderie in the team.*
- *A dapper leader: A leader who presents very well and dresses for the occasion.*

Characteristics of an Execution Leader

The attributes required for a leader to be good at Strategic Execution are:

- *Strategic and Critical Thinking,*
- *Decision-Making Skills,*
- *Business Acumen, and*
- *Innovative mindset.*

From Who is a real leader?

Value-integrated skills are critical for leaders.

Here are some of the Value Integrated Leadership skills.

- *Being a Genuine Coach*
- *Display Unbiased Empathy*
- *Deliver Impactful Communication*
- *Possess Collaborative Knowledge*
- *Make Socially Responsible Decisions and*
- *Execute Diligently*

Leaders of organizations should build a culture that encourages people to fail more often.

Provide continuous feedback to manage performance.

From The Persuasive Power of Probing

When you are solving problems for your customers, it would be advisable to lean on the two pillars of communication, Listening and Questioning, for better results. Ask those good questions, listen for great answers, and then build your robust solutions.

From Listen to Learn and Lead; So, lend your ears.

Listening to the aspirations, grievances, and pain points of your team members and customers will make you an effective leader.

From Farewells and Funerals

For leaders to transform any workplace into a harmonious and performance-driven environment, they need to:

- *Clearly articulate transparent and open feedback within teams.*
- *Offer genuine appreciation directed at individuals.*
- *Provide constructive feedback, whether positive or negative, on tasks and behaviours.*
- *These practices contribute to creating a thriving workplace culture.*

From the Brain, Heart and the Gut

- *The team learns only from the learning leaders.*
- *Leaders evolve and rise to the occasion of change.*
- *Leaders are defined by the decisions they make.*
- *Maximizing the number of right decisions made by leaders determines an organization's success.*

From Fear and Failure

- *"Fail early to succeed later."*
- *Leaders of organizations should build a culture that encourages people to fail more often.*

Negative Qualities of Leaders

Characteristics of Non-empathetic Leaders

- *The Know-it-Alls – A leader who believes that he has mastered all skills and behaves in a manner that puts down others.*
- *The Belittlers – These leaders enjoy overly criticizing and putting their team members down, even if they do exemplary work.*
- *The Control Freaks – Leaders who micromanage every single task and do not empower their teams.*
- *The Conceited Boss – Leaders who have an inflated sense of self-importance and often believe they are superior to others.*
- *Fake Listener – The leader who pretends to be paying attention during a conversation but is not genuinely engaged or interested.*
- *Selective Listener – Would listen to what they want and conveniently ignore the rest.*

Characteristics of Non-Exuberant Leaders

- *Shabbily dressed – Leaders who do not dress for the occasion.*
- *Very Serious – Does not bring energy or fun into the team.*

Characteristics of Non-execution Leaders

- *Do not set goals: Leaders who do not have a vision and do not set goals for individuals and teams.*
- *Does not follow up.*

Characteristics of Insecure Leaders

- *Lack of Confidence: An insecure leader is often hesitant and indecisive.*

- *Lack of Empathy: Insecure leaders do not empathize with their team members' pains and concerns.*
- *Micro-Management: Insecure leaders often feel the need to micromanage their employees, and this can also create a toxic work environment.*
- *Resistance to Feedback: Insecure leaders may struggle to accept critical feedback.*
- *Blaming Others: Insecure leaders are quick to blame others for their mistakes or shortcomings.*
- *Need for Control: Insecure leaders often feel the need to always be in control.*

The six deadly mistakes leaders commit.

- *Mistake No 1. Not empowering managers.*
- *Mistake No 2. Not willing to communicate with junior employees.*
- *Mistake No. 3: Not providing learning opportunities for the team.*
- *Mistake No. 4: Sweeping problems under the carpet.*
- *Mistake No. 5: Nurturing biases.*
- *Mistake No. 6: Being aggressive or passive-aggressive.*

END NOTES

Leadership Dimensions Survey, wiley.com

MBTI, myersbriggs.org

Situational Leadership, situational.com

Meditations by Marcus Aurelius (original manuscript 170-180 CE) later published in 1558-59 "The happiness of life depends on the quality of our thoughts."

Emotional Intelligence: Why It Can Matter More Than IQ (1995)– Daniel Goleman

Influence, The psychology of persuasion by Robert B Cialdini

Winning (2005) – Jack Welch; "When you were made a leader, you weren't given a crown, you were given the responsibility to bring out the best in others."

Understanding Empathy – Live2Lead Video Simon Sinek "You want to be a great leader, start with empathy and change your perspective.

The Leader Who Had No Title" (2010) – Robin Sharma, "The best leaders are masters of execution.

The Execution Premium: Linking Strategy to Operations for Competitive Advantage (Robert S Kaplan, co authored with David P. Norton), Without strong visionary leadership, no strategy will be executed effectively.

Servant Leadership: A Journey into the Nature of Legitimate Power and Greatness, Robert K Greenleaf, founder of servant leadership, the first and most important choice a leader makes is the choice to serve, without which one's capacity to lead is severely limited.

Work Management Insights: A 2020 article by MacWilson Group Limited, Strategy without execution is hallucination is mostly attributed to Thomas Alva Edison.

Be a People Person" by John C. Maxwell, Charismatic leadership is the ability to draw people in and captivate them with your vision and passion.

Socialism of My Conception, Mohandas K Gandhi, I suppose leadership at one time meant muscles; but today it means getting along with people.

Spot an Idiot Mr. J B Pritzker, The governor of Illinois, Speech at a convocation ceremony at Northwestern University. YouTube Video

The art of conversation lies in listening." is mostly attributed to Malcolm Forbes.

Hofstede Cultural Dimension; https://www.hofstede-insights.com/product/compare-countries/

ACKNOWLEDGEMENTS

Like any meaningful endeavour, the ECube Leadership book would not have become a reality without the support of a few incredible individuals who stood by me throughout the journey. I am deeply grateful to those who continuously believed in me.

- **Dr Annie Jacob (Director, KCG Tech, Hindustan Group of Institution)**, for her invaluable feedback and enriching conversations on my blogs and the psychometric tool.
- **Listle Joy (Sales Leader @ LinkedIn)** for constantly checking in on the book's progress and keeping me motivated.
- **Nandakumar, B (Principal, Business Consultant @ MavensBMG)** for being a guiding mentor.
- **Ramanathan. H (Executive Director – Executive Education, KREA University)** for being my guide in behavioural training and psychometric analysis
- **Vijaykumar R, (Financial Consultant)** for encouraging me to pursue certification in coaching and training.
- **Vinod Solomon (Secretary General @ The Southern India Chamber of Commerce)**, for inspiring me to pursue the dream of authoring a book.

And to all the leaders whose examples inspired me to write this book.